MW00593452

HOLD ON WITH A BULLDOG GRIP

James Reid Lambdin, 1868, oil on canvas.
On loan at the Ulysses S. Grant Presidential Library
from James Small, Las Vegas, Nevada.

HOLD ON WITH A BULLDOG GRIP

★ ★ ★ ★ *A Short Study of* ★ ★ ★ ★

ULYSSES S. GRANT

John F. Marszalek, David S. Nolen,

Louie P. Gallo, and Frank J. Williams

With an afterword by Mark E. Keenum
President of Mississippi State University

University Press of Mississippi / Jackson

The University Press of Mississippi is the scholarly publishing agency of
the Mississippi Institutions of Higher Learning: Alcorn State University,
Delta State University, Jackson State University, Mississippi State University,
Mississippi University for Women, Mississippi Valley State University,
University of Mississippi, and University of Southern Mississippi.

www.upress.state.ms.us

The University Press of Mississippi is a member
of the Association of University Presses.

Unless otherwise indicated, all images are courtesy of the
Bultema-Williams Collection of Ulysses S. Grant Photographs and Prints,
Ulysses S. Grant Presidential Library, Mississippi State University.

First printing 2019
∞

Library of Congress Cataloging-in-Publication Data

Names: Marszalek, John F., 1939– author. | Nolen, David S., author. |
Gallo, Louie P., author. | Williams, Frank J., author. | Keenum, Mark E.,
author of afterword.
Title: Hold on with a bulldog grip : a short study of Ulysses S. Grant /
John F. Marszalek David S. Nolen Louie P. Gallo Frank J. Williams With
an afterword by Mark E. Keenum.
Description: Jackson : University Press of Mississippi, [2019] |
Includes bibliographical references and index. |
Identifiers: LCCN 2018054786 (print) | LCCN 2018056999 (ebook) | ISBN
9781496824127 (epub single) | ISBN 9781496824103 (epub institutional) | ISBN
9781496824134 (pdf single) | ISBN 9781496824141 (pdf institutional) | ISBN
9781496824110 (cloth : alk. paper)
Subjects: LCSH: Grant, Ulysses S. (Ulysses Simpson), 1822–1885. | Generals—
United States—Biography. | Presidents—United States—Biography. | LCGFT:
Biographies. | Informational works.
Classification: LCC E672 (ebook) | LCC E672 .M33 2019 (print) | DDC
973.8/2092 [B]—dc23
LC record available at https://lccn.loc.gov/2018054786

British Library Cataloging-in-Publication Data available

CONTENTS

PLAQUE OUTSIDE OF THE
ULYSSES S. GRANT PRESIDENTIAL LIBRARY

4th Floor, Mitchell Memorial Library
November 30, 2017

Upon the July 2008 death of original Ulysses S. Grant
Association Executive Director, John Y. Simon, USGA
President, Rhode Island Chief Justice Frank J. Williams,
asked retired Mississippi State University Professor,
Dr. John F. Marszalek, to serve as USGA's new Executive
Director. With the cooperation of the USGA Board
of Directors and the MSU Administration, Williams
accomplished the transfer of USGA and its holdings to
MSU through an agreement over the telephone with
MSU Libraries Dean Frances N. Coleman. MSU
President Mark E. Keenum and USGA signed the
legal documentation in January 2009. In 2012, USGA
established the Ulysses S. Grant Presidential Library.

The donation of the Frank J. and Virginia Williams Collection of Lincolniana was made in June 2017 by Rhode Island
Supreme Court Chief Justice (ret.) Frank J. Williams and his
wife Virginia. The Lincoln gallery is located next to the gallery for the Grant Presidential Library.

INTRODUCTION

What do you think of when you hear the name Ulysses S. Grant? A few facts may come to mind: that he was a general during the Civil War, that he was president of the United States, or that his face is on the fifty-dollar bill. Others are likely to think of things they have been told about him: that he was a drunk, that he was a butcher, or that he was a corrupt president.

In this volume, the authors will present facts about Grant to help you get to know who he actually was. The first chapter gives you an overview of his life, from humble birth to tragic death. The remaining chapters highlight moments in his life that will help you understand more about the character of the man and get beyond the legends and myths about this fabled American general and president. You will have a chance to learn about his early life and his struggles in college. You will also learn about his friendship with other American icons like Mark Twain and Abraham Lincoln, the latter urging him at one point in the Civil War to "Hold on with a bulldog grip." This book explores rumors about his drinking and examines the realities of his military career and presidency. It also discusses how Grant went from being a slaveholder to being one of the most aggressive proponents of African American civil rights in his era. You will even have a chance to learn about the fascinating connections between Ulysses S. Grant and Stephen D. Lee, the first president of Mississippi State University, which foreshadowed the eventual relationship between the university and the Grant Presidential Library.

One of Grant's nineteenth-century critics once remarked after getting to know him that "My whole opinion of old USG has changed wonderfully . . . I can see now how he had friends who stuck to him through thick and thin."[1] In Grant's day, those who got to know him found things about him that they appreciated. The authors hope that you will find in this book a new appreciation of his tragic and triumphant story.

ONE

BIOGRAPHICAL SKETCH
OF ULYSSES S. GRANT

★ ★ ★ ★

In Washington, DC, directly in front of the United States Capitol and overlooking the National Mall, stands a huge equestrian statue. The man atop the horse has been afforded a position of honor among the many monuments to Founding Fathers and American icons like Washington and Jefferson. Who is this man? He is Ulysses S. Grant, the Civil War general and Reconstruction president who was adored by people all over the world during his lifetime, but who has also been belittled by subsequent generations as a drunk, a butcher on the battlefield, and a corrupt politician. So, then, what is the truth? Grant began as a humble boy growing up on the American frontier and ended with the entire nation—both North and South—grieving his death. This chapter provides an overview of his life story and highlights the themes and events in his life that will be explored in greater detail in the chapters to follow.[1]

Born in 1822, Grant, nicknamed Ulys, was not wealthy. His father, Jesse, was a tanner by profession and provided a comfortable life for his family. Ulys, the oldest of six children, worked in the tannery, but he hated the experience, tolerating, as best he could, the smells and slaughter of the animals whose hides were turned into leather products.

Ulys preferred to work on his father's lands. He drove wagon loads of lumber to sites around the area and also learned to tend the plow. He soon realized that horses made his life easier, and he quickly developed a talent for working with them.

As a child, he had a bad experience with a neighbor over a horse. It seemed that the eight-year-old Grant wanted to own a colt that belonged to a neighbor, one Robert Ralston. Grant's father had offered to buy the horse for $20, but Ralston insisted on $25, which Jesse Grant thought was too expensive. Ulys pleaded with his father to allow him to buy the horse for $25. Jesse said the horse was only worth $20, but then he yielded to his son's requests. He demanded one condition, however. Ulys was to offer $20 for the horse and raise it to $22.50 and $25 only if necessary. Grant agreed.

The young boy rode to Ralston's farm to bargain for the steed. He must have memorized his father's instructions, but he did not go about the bargaining in the way his father had hoped. He approached Ralston and blurted out: "Papa says I am to offer you twenty dollars for the colt, but if you won't take that, I am to offer twenty-two and a half, and if you won't take that, to give you twenty-five." Once this encounter became known, the neighborhood boys never let Ulys forget it, nor could he. He was so embarrassed by the incident that he even wrote about it in his memoirs nearly fifty years later.[2]

One day his father announced to Ulys that he had arranged for him an appointment to the United States Military Academy at West Point, New York. The young Grant was shocked and promptly insisted that he would not go, but Jesse's mind was made up.

One reason young Grant gave in so easily to his father was that he loved to travel. Traveling to the military academy on the Hudson River in New York gave him the chance to see new places. In mid-May 1839 he boarded a steamboat at Ripley, Ohio, and traveled to Pittsburgh, Pennsylvania. From there he took a canal boat to Harrisburg and then a first time trip on the railroad to Philadelphia. All the while he soaked in the scenery. At the end of May 1839, he arrived at West Point. There he discovered that his name was listed incorrectly on his official paperwork: he was listed as Ulysses S. Grant instead of his real name—Hiram Ulysses Grant. He gave in to this name change rather than returning home to have it corrected. He concluded upon entering the academy that "A military life had no charms for me, and I had not the faintest idea of staying in the army even if I should be graduated, which I did not expect."[3]

The five-foot, one-inch seventeen-year-old cadet quickly grew unhappy with the West Point curriculum. He never read his lessons over more than once, instead reading every novel he could get his hands on. When Congress debated a bill to abolish West Point, Grant hoped that it would pass so he could go home. But the legislation was not enacted, which meant that he had to stay there until he graduated.[4]

By the time he graduated in 1843, he had grown to a height of five feet, seven inches. Eager to see what others, especially the young women of Ohio, thought of him in his new army uniform, he hurried home. He soon lost his taste for finery, however. In his new outfit he rode a horse to Cincinnati and encountered a child in the street wearing a set of filthy, torn clothes. The child took one look at Grant and yelled out, "Soldier! Will you work? No, sir-ee; I'll sell my shirt first!!" The child's mocking response to Grant's fine new uniform stuck in the young soldier's memory, and Grant never put much stock in fine clothing again.[5]

His first assignment after graduation was with the Fourth United States Infantry Regiment at Jefferson Barracks outside St. Louis, Missouri, close to the plantation (White Haven) of his West Point roommate, Frederick Dent. Dent often invited Grant to visit his family, and the next thing he knew, Grant had fallen in love with Julia Dent, Fred's younger sister. The older Frederick Dent, the father who cultivated an image as a Southern planter, was not happy about Grant's courting of his daughter, because he did not want her to become an army officer's wife. Then, Grant received orders to go with his unit into the Mexican-American War.

The orders upset Grant, and he worried that he might not see Julia again. He finagled a leave of absence, climbed on his horse, and raced toward the Dent home. Between Jefferson Barracks and the Dent plantation was Gravois Creek, which was dry most of the year but now was a raging torrent. As he remembered it some forty years later, "One of my superstitions had always been when I started to go anywhere, or to do anything, not to turn back, or stop until the thing intended was accomplished. . . . So I struck into the stream, and in an instant the horse was swimming and I being carried down by the current. I headed the horse towards the other bank and soon reached it, wet through and without other clothes on that side of the stream." He arrived soaking wet at the Dent home, where and he and Julia shyly discussed their future. They decided to marry once his army tour was over, which meant that the actual marriage did not take place until several years later on August 22, 1848. His family, who had long held antislavery views, did not attend the wedding, because Ulys was marrying the daughter of a slaveholder.[6]

The marriage resulted in four children: Frederick Dent Grant, Ulysses S. Grant Jr. (Buck), Ellen Grant (Nellie), and Jesse R. Grant. Unhappy separation was a standard part of regular army life, with Ulys often having to leave his wife and children with his parents or hers while he was stationed in far-off locations. He suffered through depression and allegedly sometimes used alcohol to deal with his loneliness. According to some sources, his drinking got so bad in California's isolated Fort Humboldt that his commanding officer there forced him to resign his army commission in 1854. He returned to the St. Louis area and failed at a number of occupations, including farming, real estate, the lumber industry, and finally what he particularly hated: working in the tanning business. Eventually his father gave him a position in his leather goods store in Galena, Illinois, but Ulys was miserable. His father believed that Ulys was a complete failure in life and that his wife, as a slaveholder, was an inferior bride for his son. Grant continued to view himself as a failure, and so did his family, neighbors, and friends.

The coming of the Civil War looked like a great opportunity for the West Point graduate and Mexican-American War veteran. But such did not prove to be the case at the start of the war. Grant, because of rumors about his drinking, was kept out of an appropriate army position. He only made it into the army in fact when the governor of Illinois needed someone who could do paperwork to take over the state's confused records. Grant only received command of an infantry unit, the Twenty-First Illinois Volunteer Regiment, because the original commander failed at disciplining the troops. Soon after, President Abraham Lincoln elevated Grant to a brigadier general's post in exchange for the support of Congressman Elihu Washburne of Galena, Illinois.

In spite of Grant's unremarkable pre–Civil War military record, his talents for strategy and military organization shone through, and he moved quickly into the higher ranks of the Union army. His successes at Forts Henry and Donelson, Shiloh, Vicksburg, and Chattanooga launched him to national fame and in March 1864 led to his promotion to head all Union armies. His victory during the Virginia Campaign resulted in his becoming, along with Lincoln, one of the saviors of the Union. After Lincoln's untimely death, Grant's stature as an iconic figure of the Civil War only increased. His kindness in presenting generous terms of surrender to Robert E. Lee and the Confederate Army of Northern Virginia at Appomattox Court House in April 1865 made him one of the most popular individuals in post–Civil War American society.[7]

It thus made sense that Grant came to be the only possible Republican candidate for the American presidency in 1868. He won that year and again in 1872, and today is renowned as a strong advocate for African American civil rights. In fact Grant became the only president in the one hundred years between Abraham Lincoln and Lyndon B. Johnson to work at ensuring equal civil rights for African Americans. He worked to squash the Ku Klux Klan, and he tried to bring about economic salvation for the nation. There was widespread corruption during his time in the Executive Mansion, but his honesty and personal integrity remained intact.[8]

After his two terms in office he became the first president in American history to tour the world. What started out as a holiday jaunt with his family in 1877 developed into a trip in which Grant represented American democracy all over the globe. He became recognized as a world leader. Grant's tour of Europe, Asia, and Africa set the tone for American engagement in those regions into the twentieth century.[9]

When Grant returned to the United States after his prolonged and productive trip, friends and supporters backed him for an unprecedented third term as president in 1880. Those who supported him were unsuccessful in their campaign, and he did not win a third term.

Tragedy then plagued the last years of his life. His business partner Ferdinand Ward, the so-called "Wizard of Wall Street," was engaged in fraud, which left Grant bankrupt when it was discovered. The only way to ensure that Julia and his family would be financially healthy once he died was to write magazine articles about his Civil War exploits. Then he agreed to write his memoirs for Charles L. Webster and Company (Mark Twain's own publishing house) as a way to raise funds for Julia's financial well-being.

The final crushing blow was his development of throat, tongue, and tonsillar cancer, due no doubt to his being a long-time cigar smoker. Had he lived in the twenty-first century, modern medicine might have saved him, but in the 1880s when he fought the disease, the only possible medical regimen was to deaden the pain through a mixture of water and drugs. Although doctors could provide temporary relief from the pain, he suffered terribly until his death. His funeral was one of the largest in American history to this day. The mausoleum he shares with Julia is the largest tomb in North America.[10]

For a time after his tragic death Grant was recognized as one of the great names in American history. Then in the early twentieth century, historians and writers unfairly and inaccurately cast him down as a military butcher, a drunk, and one of the most corrupt presidents of all time. In the second decade of the twenty-first century, Grant is once again recognized as a major military leader, an important American president, and one of the most significant Americans ever to live.

Often, when people have visited Grant's monument in Washington, they cannot believe its grandeur. But the more they learn about this man, the more they realize how accurate a depiction it is of his greatness. Read on in this book and learn more about Grant's successes and his worthiness to have such a magnificent memorial standing in his honor.

TWO

COLLEGE LIFE

★ ★ ★ ★

In the summer of 1839 seventeen-year-old Ulysses Grant found himself far from home. He reported to the United States Military Academy in West Point, New York, as a new cadet and found a host of challenges facing him: his name was wrong on his official paperwork, older students hazed their younger peers, and he hated being there so much that he even wished that the government would shut down the school. On top of all those challenges, he confronted a problem that has plagued college students for generations: French class. He later recalled in his memoirs, "I did not take hold of my studies with avidity, in fact I rarely ever read over a lesson the second time during my entire cadetship."[1]

His own stated lack of enthusiasm for his studies has reinforced the popular conception that he was a bad student who finished last, or near the bottom, in his class. He has been characterized as someone who just barely scraped by and possessed no impressive qualities or traits. But what is the real story?

Grant was born in Point Pleasant, Ohio, in 1822, and spent much of his time growing up in the nearby town of Georgetown, where his family moved when he was young. When he reached school age, his parents, Jesse and Hannah, made sure he regularly attended local schools. Young Grant, however, did not prove himself particularly adept in primary school, developing a reputation as an average student. Nonetheless, he did show some promise in one area: he was consistently good at mathematics.[2]

In Grant's day the normal process for young men was to work with their fathers and learn the family business as an apprentice. For Grant this presented a daunting challenge. His father Jesse was engaged in many different business ventures but was primarily a tanner, turning animal hides into leather in a laborious process that was bloody, smelly, and overall disgusting to young Ulysses. The boy hated the sight of blood and dead animals, not to mention the overpowering smells of the process. He once remarked to his father, "Father, this tanning is not the kind of work I like. I'll work at it though . . . if you wish me to, until I am twenty-one; but you may depend upon it, I'll never work a day at it after that."[3]

Instead of tanning, Grant expressed interest in other types of work. He loved working with animals—especially horses—and spent much of his boyhood helping out on his family's farm. He told his father that he might enjoy farming, but that was not an easy life: it required significant resources in land and animals. The farmer's success depended on his own effort as well as uncontrollable factors like weather. Too many variables could ruin a man working in agriculture. And Jesse did not have the resources to help his son get established in that profession.

As with many young men of that era, a life on the river also appealed to the young Grant with its promise of adventure, money, and travel to distant places. Young Grant had already traveled around his corner of the world a good bit during his boyhood, visiting places seventy miles from home. Time and again he had proven himself trustworthy and responsible in his errands. Nonetheless, Jesse did not favor the idea of his son living a life on the river. He knew that such a body of water, along with all its commercial benefits, also presented opportunities for immorality to young men far from home. Thus neither of Ulysses's stated interests matched with his father's hopes for his future.[4]

But there was one other possibility that Ulysses had mentioned: getting an education. So Jesse, who prized education, set his sights on getting his son into college. In the early nineteenth century a college education meant the opportunity to become something other than a tradesman, to receive training for a profession such as medicine or law. Jesse knew that a college education would provide his son with more opportunities than either farming or work on the river, but entrance into college and its accompanying cost could be difficult for a man of modest prosperity like himself.

The solution presented itself in 1839. A number of local boys from Georgetown had completed their studies tuition-free at the United States Military Academy (USMA) and gone on to successful careers in the army and then later as private citizens. Jesse decided that a free college education was too good to pass up. He decided to pursue an appointment to the academy for his son Ulysses.[5]

Just like today, entrance into the USMA required a congressional appointment (in addition to meeting the admission criteria). One unanticipated complication was that Senator Thomas Morris, whom Jesse initially wrote to in an effort to get his son appointed, had waived his right to appoint a cadet and was therefore unable to nominate Ulysses. But Senator Morris also provided Jesse with some interesting news: there was a vacant appointment for a cadet from Jesse's own congressional district. Unknown to most people in Georgetown, Bart Bailey, the most recent appointee to the USMA from the area, had resigned, opening up a vacancy for a new cadet. Morris suggested that Jesse contact the congressman from his district, Thomas Hamer.[6] But that was bad news for Jesse: years before, he and Hamer had had a falling out over politics, and their close friendship had cooled.[7] Would Hamer now come to the aid of the family and be willing to offer his support to Ulysses? Jesse decided his only option was to write Hamer to find out.

Hamer apparently viewed the letter requesting an appointment to the USMA for Ulysses as an opportunity to mend fences, so he quickly agreed and wrote out a letter of appointment on behalf of Jesse Grant's son. But he made one important mistake: Hamer did not get the boy's name right. Jesse's firstborn son's name was Hiram Ulysses, with family and friends calling him by his middle name. Hamer, however, wrote out an appointment for Ulysses S. Grant, not Hiram Ulysses Grant. Where the "S" came from, we do not know. Perhaps Hamer remembered that Hannah Grant's maiden name was Simpson and mistakenly thought that was Ulysses's middle name. At any rate, Ulysses S. Grant became the name in the official paperwork of the boy from Georgetown, Ohio, appointed to the USMA.[8]

Jesse's plans were thus set in motion, and their success would ultimately impact Ulysses in profound ways. In later years, Jesse claimed that his son was enthusiastic about attending the academy, but Ulysses recorded a different version of events in his memoirs. According to Ulysses, during the Christmas season of 1838, Jesse informed him that he was pursuing an appointment for him. "What appointment?" asked Ulysses. "To West Point; I have applied for it," answered his father. "But I won't go," said Ulysses. The younger Grant's protest fell on deaf ears. As Ulysses neatly summed it up, the decision had already been made by his father. "He said he thought I would, *and I thought so too, if he did*."[9]

Ulysses left home for West Point, New York, in 1839. One of his concerns about heading off to the USMA had centered on his name. He knew that as a first-year cadet he would face the ridicule of older students as part of the initiation process at the academy. He was small for his age at only five feet, one inch tall and roughly 117 pounds, but his initials placed an even bigger target on his back: Hiram Ulysses Grant, or HUG. His concern was such that he had already begun reversing his first two initials and signing letters as "Ulysses H. Grant," hoping to avoid the dreaded acronym and the accompanying unflattering nicknames that would undoubtedly follow.[10]

When he arrived at the academy, however, he found his predicament already solved by Congressman Hamer's earlier mistake: there was no Hiram Ulysses Grant or Ulysses H. Grant on the roster. There was only a "Ulysses S. Grant." This ultimately became his legal name for the rest of his life. His new initials resulted in a more livable series of nicknames: the other cadets called him "Uncle Sam Grant," eventually shortening it to just Sam.[11] Later on, during the Civil War, his nickname of "Unconditional Surrender Grant" became shorthand for his reputation as a hard-nosed fighter.

According to his memoirs, Grant's unwillingness to attend the USMA primarily stemmed from his own concerns about his qualifications to enter the academy. He confessed that he was worried that he would not be able to do the academic work to be successful there, and he would have rather not even attempted it than to have tried and failed.[12] While some cadets relished the rigors of military life and adhered to the minute details necessary to excel, Grant did not enjoy the life of drill and study. He recorded in his memoirs years later that "A military life had no charms for me, and I had not the faintest idea of staying in the army even if I should be graduated, which I did not expect."[13]

Yet Grant made it through four years of study at West Point, coming into contact with many future American military leaders. Among the cadets who were also there during Grant's years were William T. Sherman, George H. Thomas, James Longstreet, Don Carlos Buell, and Richard Ewell, among many others. These men all went on to play major roles in the events of the Civil War.[14]

So what became of Grant the reluctant cadet? Was he truly a poor student and an unintelligent man? Grant himself added to the lore when he wrote about his college experience in his memoirs, "I never succeeded in getting squarely at either end of my class, in any one study, during the four years. I came near it in French, artillery, infantry and cavalry tactics, and conduct."[15]

Class rank at West Point is still an important measure of a cadet's success, and it was perhaps even more important in the nineteenth century. Those graduating in the top of the class were lauded, while those graduating at the bottom of the class earned a certain notoriety. In addition, the army assigned USMA graduates their duties based on their class standing.

Looking at the *Official Register of the Officers and Cadets of the U.S. Military Academy* for the four years that Grant was at the USMA, it is clear that he was correct in his insistence that he was never clearly at the top or bottom of his class. His overall ranking (what was termed the "Order of General Merit") was consistently in the middle of his class: 27 out of 60 cadets in his first year, 24 out of 53 cadets in his second year, 20 out of 41 cadets in his third year, and finally 21 out of 39 cadets in his fourth year.[16]

As to Grant's claims in his memoirs about his class standings in his coursework, he was near the bottom of his class in French (49 out of 60 during his first year and then 44 out of 53 in his second year). In his fourth year he was nearer the middle of the class in artillery, finishing 25 out of 39 cadets. In Infantry Tactics (which he also took during his fourth year) he ranked 28 out of 39 cadets. In the "Roll of the Cadets, Arranged According to Merit In Conduct" Grant was likewise middle of the pack or slightly lower in each year: 147 out of 233 in his first year, 144 out of 219 in his second year, 157 out of 217 in his third year, and 156 out of 223 in his final year at the USMA.[17]

In spite of such mediocre grades, Cadet Grant did distinguish himself in some ways. He impressed his instructors and classmates with his ability to maneuver and jump over obstacles on horseback. While a cadet, Grant set the USMA record for high jump on a horse: five feet, six and a half inches, a record that stood until at least the 1890s.[18] In his first year at the academy, he was 16 out of 60 in mathematics. In fact he was so consistently good at math that at one point he even talked about becoming an assistant math professor.[19] Interestingly, Grant also enjoyed the art classes that he took at the USMA, producing some fine paintings and drawings during his time as a cadet.

Grant commented on his overall average performance in his memoirs:

I did not take hold of my studies with avidity, in fact I rarely ever read over a lesson the second time during my entire cadetship. I could not sit in my room doing nothing. There is a fine library connected with the Academy from which cadets can get books to read in their quarters. I devoted more time to these, than to books relating to the course of studies. Much of the time, I am sorry to say, was devoted to novels, but not those of a trashy sort. I read all of Bulwer's then published, Cooper's, Marryat's, Scott's, Washington Irving's works, Lever's, and many others that I do not now remember.[20]

Grant's memory may have failed him in this instance, as historian Ronald C. White states that the library did not collect novels at that time and did not check out books to cadets. Instead, they had to read books from the collection within the library. Therefore, Grant most likely borrowed the novels he read from other cadets, lending them books of his own in an informal book-sharing arrangement.[21]

So, was Grant truly an unintelligent man who only scraped by in the classroom? The evidence points to something different: like many reluctant students, Grant did just enough to get by in his classes and found other interests to pursue during his college years that made his experience more enjoyable. He did not study as much as he could have, and his grades reflected that. For him the rigors of a military education did not play to his strengths and interests. Overall, he was just like many college students, struggling to balance school responsibilities and leisure, all the while planning for a life and a career after graduation.

THREE

THE EVILS OF SLAVERY

★ ★ ★ ★

The historical record is unclear, but in 1858, Grant either purchased an enslaved man named William Jones or was given him by his father-in-law, Colonel Frederick Dent. As someone who grew up in an abolitionist household, Grant understood the evils of slavery, but because of his financial struggles he accepted the man nonetheless. Grant also hired two free African American men for a year at a time. The four men, including Grant, all worked alongside each other in the fields that year to expedite the farming process.[1] Despite his best efforts, Grant was unable to make a living through farming, which left him strapped for cash and in a precarious position. What was he to do with William? Would he keep him, sell him, or give him his freedom?

To better understand Grant and how his view of slavery evolved over time, one must first examine the history of slavery in the United States of America, which predated the founding of the country, and how it shaped the country's economy, culture, and views of African Americans.

Slavery became an integral part of the colonial system in North America by the middle of the 1600s.[2] By the time the United States broke free from Great Britain, racial theories about Africans that justified the slave system were already well established. Most white Americans viewed enslaved African people as subhuman and as being unable to properly take care of themselves. People of African descent were portrayed as being stupid, childlike, and savage. There was a palpable fear among most of the white community that slaves, out of irrational anger, would revolt and destroy the white way of life.[3] Physical stereotypes were also attached to enslaved Africans. The Mississippi Secession Ordinance of 1861, for example, in discussing the importance of slavery to Southern agriculture, stated that "by an imperious law of nature, none but the black race can bear exposure to the tropical sun."[4]

There was, however, notable opposition to the reprehensible institution early on in its existence. Abolitionist societies, usually started by religious groups, were common after the Revolutionary War. The Quaker community pushed for the abolition of slavery, and influential people such as Benjamin Franklin were involved in the movement. Franklin was even the president of the Pennsylvania Abolition Society. Most Northern states—including Vermont, New York, Pennsylvania, Maryland, and Connecticut—had some sort of antislavery advocacy groups.[5] In 1808 the Kentucky Abolition Society, located in a slave state bordering a free state, was founded.[6]

Ulysses S. Grant's immediate family was involved in the abolitionist movement. The death of his mother forced a young Jesse Grant, Ulysses's father, to move in with Owen Brown and his family, which included future abolitionist John Brown. Ulysses wrote about his father's relationship with John Brown in his memoirs:

I have often heard my father speak of John Brown, particularly since the events at Harper's Ferry. Brown was a boy when they lived in the same house, but he knew him afterwards, and regarded him as a man of great purity of character, of high moral and physical courage, but a fanatic and extremist in whatever he advocated.[7]

In the 1830s, Jesse wrote political articles for the *Castigator*, an abolitionist newspaper published in Georgetown, Ohio.[8] The Grant family was also close friends with Thomas Morris, who was one of the first senators to be openly against slavery. In fact Ulysses's mother, Hannah Simpson Grant, was a bridesmaid in the wedding of Morris's daughter, Julia.[9] Another Grant family member, Peter Grant, Ulysses's uncle, was an ardent abolitionist and the president of an abolitionist society in Maysville, Kentucky. Fourteen-year-old Ulysses lived with this uncle's family while attending the Maysville Seminary.[10]

Grant's family may have included outspoken abolitionists, but Ulysses, in his early years, did not identify with the movement. He was a member of a debate club while living in Maysville, and he once argued that immediate abolitionism was not practicable.[11] Perhaps it was from living in rural Ohio, or the fact that he was busy trying to make something of himself in the military, that young Ulysses was indifferent to the issue of slavery. He made this clear in an August 30, 1863, letter to his friend, Congressman Elihu Washburne. Grant asserted:

> I never was an Abolitionest, [n]ot even what could be called anti slavery, but I try to judge farely & honestly and it become patant to my mind early in the rebellion that the North & South could never live at peace with each other except as one nation, and that without Slavery. As anxious as I am to see

peace reestablished I would not therefore be willing to see any
settlemen[t] until this question is forever settled.[12]

Like the vast majority of Americans, Grant was troubled by
the possibility of disunion, which many felt was being insti-
gated by parties on both sides of the slavery issue. This may
have been the major reason why he was reluctant to con-
demn slavery more directly at that time in his life.

Another indication of Grant's indifference toward slavery in his early life was evident in his relationship with Julia
Dent. He met Julia through her brother, Fred, who was his
roommate in his final year at the United States Military
Academy in West Point, New York. Grant frequently visited
the Dent family estate, White Haven, when he was stationed
at Jefferson Barracks in St. Louis, Missouri.[13] White Haven
was an eight-hundred-acre plantation purchased by Frederick Dent in 1820. Dent frequently used the honorary title of
"colonel," which did not denote an actual military rank but
instead implied that he was a wealthy landowner and a man
of Southern nobility.[14] By 1850 the plantation had approximately thirty slaves.[15]

Julia lived on the property during most of her childhood.
Growing up, she had had her own personal slave, a young
woman also named Julia. In her memoirs, which were published nearly one hundred years after her death, Julia Dent
Grant portrayed White Haven as being a place enjoyed by
everyone, and she reinforced the Lost Cause myth of "the
happy slave."[16] In reference to the enslaved people at White
Haven, she wrote, "I think our people were very happy. . . .
My father was most kind and indulgent to his people."[17]

Despite the Dent family's proslavery views and his own
family's antislavery views, Grant still pursued Julia. At first

Colonel Dent did not approve of Julia marrying Ulysses, because he believed that it was beneath her to marry a military man. Over time, however, Grant earned the colonel's blessing. He and Julia married on August 22, 1848.[18]

During the years before the Civil War, Grant had numerous political discussions with Dent at White Haven. The Colonel constantly railed against abolitionists and legal matters that dealt with slavery, and Grant was more than willing to engage in the conversations. In a letter written on April 19, 1861, only days after the bombardment of Fort Sumter on the South Carolina coast, Grant wrote to Dent detailing his opinions about the upcoming conflict and the future of slavery:

> The times are indee[d] startling but now is the time, particularly in the border Slave states, for men to prove their love of country ... and every true patriot be for maintaining the integrity of the glorious old *Stars & Stripes*, the Constitution and the Union.[19]

He also understood that the primary cause of the war was slavery, and he asserted that the Northern states would not hesitate to end slavery if it meant keeping the Union together. Grant wrote, "In all this I can but see the doom of Slavery."[20]

As a general in the Civil War, Grant was forced to take a strong stand on slavery. He could no longer ignore the impact that slavery would have on the future of the country. He proved to be sympathetic to enslaved people who attempted to escape from bondage. He employed them as teamsters, hospital attendants, and cooks. He even paid the escaped slaves, then known as "contraband" or "freedmen," for the cotton and food that they foraged from abandoned plantations.[21] In a letter to his sister Mary in August 1862, Grant admitted, "I don't know what is to become of these poor people in the end but it is weakening the enemy to take them from them."[22]

After Lincoln issued the first Emancipation Proclamation, Grant was eager to include freed African Americans as troops into the Union army. On June 7, 1863, Grant used the Eleventh Louisiana Infantry, composed of freed African Americans, to drive out the Confederates near Milliken's Bend on the Mississippi River. This battle was one of the first times that African American troops fought during the war. Later, near the end of the war, Grant utilized black troops during the Overland Campaign in Virginia. However, he substituted an untrained white division to push the attack after the mine explosion at Petersburg, even though black troops had been trained for the task. [23]

When Grant wrote his memoirs at the end of his life, he reflected on the role slavery played in bringing on the Civil War. He wrote, "The cause of the great War of the Rebellion against the United States will have to be attributed to slavery." He also discussed how integrating African Americans into society was necessary for the future of the nation:

> The condition of the colored man within our borders may become a source of anxiety, to say the least. But he was brought to our shores by compulsion, and he now should be considered as having as good a right to remain here as any other class of our citizens.[24]

After the war, during his presidency, Grant grew to be even more accepting of African Americans and their rights as human beings. He proclaimed, "My oft expressed desire is that all citizens, white or black, native or foreign born, may be left free, in all parts of our common country, to vote, speak and act, in obedience to law, without intimidation or ostracism on account of his views, color or nativity."[25] Grant supported the passage of the Fifteenth Amendment, which gave African American men the right to vote. He also signed into law the Enforcement Acts, which were designed to protect the civil rights of African Americans and to subvert the influence of white supremacist groups, such as the Ku Klux Klan. His evolving opinion of slavery and the social question of race in America demonstrated his realization of the equality of every person. Grant was advanced in his views on race relations, and it took the nation years to embrace his vision. There would not be another piece of civil rights legislation passed for almost one hundred years after his presidency.

As for William Jones, the enslaved man given to him, Grant freed him in 1859. In the manumission document, however, Grant did not provide a reason for granting William his freedom, leaving historians to speculate on Grant's motivations to make such a seemingly selfless decision during a period of personal financial difficulty. No matter what Grant's motivations were, the freeing of William Jones highlighted how Grant's antislavery views began to take shape even before the Civil War.

FOUR

JUST A TASTE OF LIQUOR

★ ★ ★ ★

One of Grant's closest friends and mentors was John A. Rawlins, a Galena, Illinois, neighbor and his Civil War chief of staff. He is often cited as the individual who watched over Grant to make sure that he did not drink too often or too heavily. On November 17, 1863, just before the crucial Battle of Chattanooga, Rawlins grew so frustrated about Grant's alleged overdrinking that he wrote him a scathing letter: "I again appeal to you in the name of everything a friend, an honest man, and a lover of his country holds dear, to immediately desist from further tasting of liquors of any kind. . . . Two more nights like the last will find you prostrated on a sick bed unfit for duty. This must not be. You only can prevent it, and for the sake of my bleeding country and your own honor I pray God you may."[1] Clearly, in that moment, Rawlins saw Grant as a dangerous drinker. Was he?

During the nineteenth century the United States was a nation of drinkers. Consumption records indicate that Americans consumed alcohol in distilled form, in cider, wine, beer, medicine, and even in cooked food.[2] During the 1860s, although Americans did drink heavily, they were not the leading consumers of alcohol in the world. On a per capita basis, citizens of the United States drank about 2.1

gallons a year of distilled alcohol, but Swedes drank 2.6 gallons. Americans drank only .3 gallons of wine per year, while Germans drank 1.6 gallons and the French drank 26.4. Even beer drinking in the United States did not rival the numbers consumed in many European countries. Americans drank 4.2 gallons of beer a year, but England consumed 32.0 gallons, Germany 14.5, and France 5.0. In total, Americans drank some 6.6 gallons of alcohol per year, a substantial amount, but not world-leading.[3]

In the nineteenth century many Americans believed that people became drunk because they could not discipline or control themselves, or were simply immoral. A large number of temperance organizations sprang up during these years to try to demonstrate the immoral basis of drinking and to shame drinkers into abstaining. In those years practically no one believed that alcoholism was a disease, so they looked down on those who displayed any propensity toward drunkenness or were suspected of any such activities.

Since getting drunk was considered immoral, it was quickly linked to the nineteenth-century problems of abuse of women, neglect of children, and the inability to find or hold on to a job. The apparent breakdown of the family structure within a similar crumbling of society created fear among Americans about overuse of alcoholic beverages. Something had to be done to prevent drunkenness from destroying the nation.

Because the nineteenth century saw the development of religious reform movements, it made sense that this fervor be turned against alcohol. All sorts of temperance societies came into being, often so entwined with other reform movements as to make any real progress against drinking nearly impossible. For example, the maintenance of the Sabbath

(Sabbatarianism) became the be-all for solving society's problems, so temperance no longer stood out as the major solution. Yet the American Temperance Society came into being in 1826, gaining momentum from the overall moral rebirth. By the late 1830s temperance advocates numbered between four and five million American people, with temperance societies developing all over the nation.[4]

The argument over whether to prohibit or to moderate alcoholic consumption quickly became the main debate. In the 1850s, as the argument raged, thirteen states and territories passed laws allowing localities to determine how to regulate alcohol consumption. Local option came into vogue. At the same time, the movement to keep the Sabbath holy and avoid secular activities pushed through laws prohibiting the sale of any kind of alcohol on Sundays.

Increasingly temperance came to mean abstinence. At the same time, Americans came to believe that drunkenness or appearing slovenly was a mark of especial moral weakness. Women of course were not supposed to drink, but males who displayed any weakness toward what was often called "Demon Rum" were seen as unmanly. They were to drink moderately if at all, and they were never to display any indication of over-drinking. Men were never to appear disheveled or speak with a slurred tongue. Drinking thus became a sign of immorality. It was only with the growth of the medical profession and other more modern insights that American society came to understand that alcoholism was a disease and not a weakness.[5]

It was within this context that Ulysses S. Grant lived and matured. Like most members of American society, he drank alcohol at times and did look unkempt. His lack of success in business also created suspicion that he had some sort of weakness (i.e., drunkenness). In spite of later rumors, it was common knowledge that he drank only infrequently while a student at West Point and very little during the Mexican-American War.[6]

The first real indication that Grant had a drinking problem occurred during his 1849–1850 winter in Detroit. There, as a young, newly married officer, he experienced the cold frontier post without his wife, who was back in Missouri preparing to give birth to their first child. Grant turned to his Methodist pastor, Dr. George Taylor, for help. Taylor, a firm believer in temperance, told Grant that he must avoid all drink, so Grant took the pledge never to drink again. He realized that he had a drinking problem, not in the amount that he consumed but in the fact that he could not handle alcohol at all. Clearly he was determined to battle what he came to believe was a moral weakness in himself. When his military career took him to Sackett's Harbor, New York, he helped establish a temperance organization there. He became so convinced that temperance was the way to defeat his propensity that, for a time, he even wore temperance regalia to display his beliefs.[7]

In January 1854 Grant experienced a bout with drinking that would haunt him for the rest of his life and long after his death. He arrived without wife and family at Fort Humboldt near Eureka, California, an isolated post, with the troops stationed there having practically nothing to do. Making things even worse, Colonel Robert C. Buchanan commanded this army post in the middle of an unpopulated wilderness. Buchanan was a stickler for military discipline and was in fact universally known as uncompromising.

The young officer found the fort where he was stationed to be lonely without his wife, Julia, and he also suffered because he hardly received any mail from her. Contact with local tribes was less frequent than at other posts, so when Grant's military company did anything military, it seemed pointless. Grant hated being there. Missing his wife and children and having nothing to do, he drank heavily.

He desperately wanted to follow Julia's desire that he not drink. Still he began to drink more and more. He became ill from drinking, but he kept at it anyway. It seemed to others that he did not drink as much as many of the other officers at the isolated fort did, but his reaction to alcohol was worse. He could not hold his drinks, so his appearance grew ever worse, and the drinking only led to more depression.

Then there was Buchanan. The army colonel grew furious as he watched Grant sinking into a pit of alcoholism. Finally, one day when Grant appeared especially drunk, Buchanan exploded. He told his adjutant to confront Grant and tell him that if he did not resign from the army immediately, Buchanan would court-martial him on the spot. Worried about the embarrassment such legal action would inflict on Julia, Grant decided to resign. He left the army and returned to Missouri to try to begin a new life.[8]

Home with his wife and family, Grant stayed away from alcohol. Still the word of his resignation spread throughout the small peace-time army. Grant was labeled a drunk who resigned his army commission because of his drunkenness. He achieved so little success in his subsequent civilian life that, when he tried to rejoin the army at the onset of the Civil War, the drinking rumors followed him and apparently helped prevent his reentrance. It was only because of the political influence of Galena, Illinois, friends like Congressman Elihu Washburne that he finally gained command of a Civil War regiment and began climbing the ladder of promotion.[9]

Yet the rumors persisted. His commanding officer, General Henry W. Halleck, went out of his way to find fault with Grant and feed rumors about him. Halleck insisted that Grant drank to excess, but he never provided any evidence of Grant's drinking.[10]

Notable general William T. Sherman and Grant were fast friends during the war, and Sherman admitted later that Grant was no stranger to alcohol, stating, "We all knew at the time that Genl. Grant would occasionally drink too much . . . [but] when anything was pending he was invariably abstinent of drink."[11]

Perhaps the most famous of the accusations against Grant came from newspaper reporter Sylvanus Cadwallader, who insisted that he had seen Grant severely drunk on a boat trip during the 1863 Vicksburg campaign. In fact Cadwallader was not even on the trip he described. Yet he insisted that the story he told about Grant was true, and contemporaries and many later historians have taken the reporter's accusations at face value.[12]

There are countless examples of Grant passing up a drink because he understood that even a small sip could hurt him. In fact during his time in the White House, there is no indication of him ever being under the influence. He seemed to have fought a victorious battle over something that had tormented him throughout his early years. As modern historian Ron Chernow asserts, Grant was no longer drinking by the time he became president.[13]

And so, was Grant a drunk? It is fairer to say that he had a low tolerance for alcohol and was a binge drinker who sometimes drank more than he could handle. Perhaps Mary Livermore, an important member of the United States Sanitary Commission, put it best. She insisted that, while she was serving along the Mississippi River, many Union generals drank too much. But she concluded that "Neither was General Grant a drunkard,—that was immediately apparent to us."[14]

Perhaps, too, Grant was just another example of a Civil War general who used alcohol to deal with the horrors of war. As for John A. Rawlins, he was a temperance advocate, who in his relationship with Grant, carried on a personal crusade against alcohol. The letter addressed to Grant that begins this chapter is a broad indictment of Grant's drinking, but the fact of the matter is that Rawlins never sent it. He later wrote on the outside of the letter, "This letter was written hastily with a view to handing to the one to whom it is addressed but on reflection it was not given to him, but I talked to him upon the subject to which it relates, which had the desired effect."[15] Rawlins concluded that the problem had been resolved.

FIVE

FIGHTING THE WAR

★ ★ ★ ★

In the summer of 1861 Colonel Ulysses S. Grant and his regiment had been ordered to pursue Confederate Brigadier
General Thomas Harris in Missouri. "As we approached the
brow of the hill from which it was expected we could see
Harris's camp, and possibly find his men ready formed to
meet us," he wrote later, "my heart kept getting higher and
higher until it felt to me that it was in my throat."[1] Grant was
overwhelmed with fear, but what lesson did he learn that day
that influenced him throughout the conflict?

To understand the importance of that experience early
in the war, it is helpful to examine the characteristics that
Grant displayed as a commander. After being promoted to
brigadier general in August 1861, he became a national hero
when he captured Forts Henry and Donelson in February
1862. But he would face potential defeat later that spring. In
April 1862 the Confederates caught him off guard at Pitts-
burg Landing/Shiloh on the first day of the two-day battle
and drove his forces practically into the Tennessee River.
A subordinate, William Tecumseh Sherman, approached
him the night after the first day's battle. Grant's forces were
pinned against the river, and the rain poured down severely.
He said, "Well, Grant, we've had the devil's own day, haven't

we?" He thought that his commander would immediately order a retreat. Instead Grant demonstrated to Sherman one of the traits that marked his military philosophy, responding, "Yes, lick 'em tomorrow though." And that was precisely what happened. The next morning Grant's forces went on the attack, pushed the Confederates off the battlefield, and won an important victory. Grant believed in always moving forward and doggedly pursuing victory.[2]

An even better example of this characteristic of determination became obvious at one of the most important battles of the entire war: Vicksburg, Mississippi, along the Mississippi River. It was clear to both sides that Vicksburg had to be captured. Lincoln put it best when he said: "Vicksburg is the key. The war can never be brought to a close until the key is in our pocket."[3] If the Federals could capture this city, they would control the Mississippi River, cut the Confederacy in half, and prevent supplies from the Trans-Mississippi West reaching the Confederate military in the East.

But it would take fearless forward movement, and it was not that easy. At Fort Donelson and Shiloh, Grant had to overcome difficult odds to snatch victory from near defeat. The odds were again stacked against him: he had to contend with the weather, the river, the terrain, and back-biting Union generals and politicians, let alone the Confederate forces.[4]

As Federal leaders debated over how best to deal with Vicksburg, Major General John McClernand of Illinois convinced President Abraham Lincoln that he should form a new military force from volunteers McClernand recruited in the lower Midwest. Once he had these men in tow, the plan was for McClernand to move down the Mississippi River from Memphis to take Vicksburg. Grant was shocked and dismayed at this development, which would have undermined his efforts to capture Vicksburg. Undeterred by the president's action, Grant made an immediate decision. He told Sherman to take all of McClernand's troops that came to him as his own. He was to immediately move against Vicksburg and take it before McClernand arrived on the scene and took command by virtue of seniority.[5]

In support of Sherman, Grant told him that he would move through the center of Mississippi, via Grenada, while Sherman steadily steamed down the Mississippi River. The idea was for Sherman to attack Vicksburg from the river, while Grant attacked it on land from the East.

This was a plan that made sense. But then in December 1862 Confederate General Earl Van Dorn destroyed Grant's supply base at Holly Springs, Mississippi, and Grant could not make it to Vicksburg. Sherman's advance also faltered at Chickasaw Bayou. The well-conceived plan was proving to be a failure, and as the new year of 1863 began, Grant was no closer to taking Vicksburg than he had been before. He might easily have quit and, as Sherman suggested, gone back to Memphis to restart the attack on Vicksburg from there. Instead he stayed in the watery surroundings of Vicksburg and plotted other ways to reach his object. He kept pressing in all directions, demonstrating no fear.

Grant first tried a series of difficult maneuvers that most other generals would never have tried. He attempted to build a canal across the peninsula above Vicksburg where the Mississippi River made a horseshoe turn. The canal did not work. He then cut a gap in the Mississippi River levee to allow boats to travel through Lake Providence and other water ways. Once again he failed. He purposefully tried to get troops on solid dry ground below Vicksburg, but the so-called Yazoo Pass expedition ran into Confederate Fort

Pemberton at the merger of the Tallahatchie and Yalobusha rivers and was forced back. Grant then tried and failed with the Steele's Bayou expedition led by Admiral David D. Porter's naval forces.[6]

Importantly, though, Grant kept trying scheme after scheme. He continued to plow forward. He remained governed by what, in his memoirs, he called his "superstition," never to turn back once he had decided to go somewhere or do something.[7] Though his efforts kept failing, he still showed no fear.

Almost in desperation, Grant met with Admiral Porter, and they agreed to cooperate on a new plan. Porter would send gunboats and transports south down the river, past the cannons of Vicksburg. At the same time, Sherman's corps would do an enormous feint against Hayne's Bluff, in the area near where Sherman had failed at Chickasaw Bayou in December 1862. Grant's army also marched south on the west side of the Mississippi River until the force was across from Grand Gulf. There the boats shelled this installation, tried to disable it, and served as ferry boats for the army troops moving from the west to the east side of the river. It was a dangerous plan, but, unlike other Union generals, Grant was a bold strategist who was willing to take chances.

Like the earlier ones this plan was also a failure. Grand Gulf would not fall to the Navy's bombardment, so something else had to be tried. Fortunately a local enslaved man told Grant about an excellent place to cross to the east side of the river and move north through the area. Grant did not allow nineteenth-century prejudice about the supposed unreliability of African Americans to impede him. He marched his forces further south until they reached a point across the river from Bruinsburg, Mississippi. There he would try to get the navy to ferry his soldiers across the river at the spot the black man had suggested.

This time, Grant's plan worked. His refusal to let fear of failure paralyze him landed him on dry ground below Vicksburg. Sherman's feint was also successful, and he quickly raced back to Grant's main force. McClernand's Midwestern recruits also had joined Grant's army, and Benjamin Grierson's cavalry raid through the eastern side of Mississippi was progressing. Confederate Generals John Pemberton and Joseph E. Johnston, along with Confederate President Jefferson Davis, were all trying to direct Grant's opposition, but the result was confusion rather than leadership. Johnston even thought it was too late for him to help preserve Vicksburg; Jefferson Davis disliked Johnston, and he was telling Pemberton that he should hold on to Vicksburg, no matter what Johnston said.[8]

As always Grant moved with appropriate haste, going on the offensive as soon as he could and rocking the Confederates back on their heels. He moved his army northeast from Bruinsburg, keeping his left flank on the Big Black River. Doing what no general was supposed to do, he daringly placed his force between one Confederate army in the west and another in the east. He sent his army east where he captured Jackson, Mississippi, and drove Johnston further out of the action. Then he turned quickly and moved directly against Vicksburg. He defeated the Confederates at Champion Hill, crossed the Big Black River, and forced Pemberton to fall back into Vicksburg. Grant moved against the city on the bluffs and surrounded it. He tried two separate attacks on the entrenched Southerners, hoping to break through and to end the campaign quickly, but he failed both times. Yet, in spite of these setbacks, he continued to push forward.

Grant decided to clamp down on the city with a siege, cutting off supplies to the city. Slowly but surely he starved Vicksburg and the Confederate army into submission. Trench warfare, the digging of approaches forward and laterally, the broiling Mississippi sun, and continual cannon fire lobbing shells into the city from Union boats on the river made life miserable for everyone. Civilians began to live in caves, food became scarce, and hope of relief seemed to diminish with every day. Union forces were winning.

Finally, on July 4, 1863, Pemberton had no choice but to surrender. Grant had won a great victory. He accepted the Confederate capitulation, and then when it came time to decide what to do with Pemberton's defeated army, he did something that once again no other general would have done. He sent the Southern soldiers home, knowing that on their way they would tell the Confederate civilians of the dire straits of their Confederate army. He ended that army's existence as a fighting force by paroling them all, sending them home and away from the front lines. Since this happened on July 4, the anniversary of the Union's formation in 1776 and the day after Robert E. Lee was defeated in Gettysburg, Pennsylvania, the war, not just the key, was in Grant's and Lincoln's pockets. Building on this success, Grant came to the relief of a Union army in Chattanooga in November 1863. Not long after that Lincoln called him to Washington to become lieutenant general and commander of all Union forces in 1864.[9]

Another hallmark of Grant's strategy then became evident. He emphasized the overall theaters of war not just individual places or battles. Instead of fighting piecemeal and allowing the Confederates to shift their forces to meet any Union attack, Grant called for all the Union armies to be on the attack together everywhere, all the time, so as to take full advantage of Federal numerical superiority. In Virginia, Union general George G. Meade and the Army of the Potomac would drive toward Richmond, Virginia; Franz Sigel would move up the Shenandoah Valley and west toward the Confederate capital of Richmond. Benjamin Butler would drive north from Fortress Monroe on the Virginia coast. At the same time, Sherman would march from Chattanooga, Tennessee, toward Savannah, Georgia, while Nathaniel Banks would take Mobile, Alabama, and push east.[10] While these generals waged destructive warfare, Grant kept constant pressure on Robert E. Lee in Virginia's wilderness and beyond. The results were battles with huge casualties. Many soldiers on both sides lost their lives, but steadily Grant ground down Lee's army. Lee saw his army grow smaller and smaller until not enough men were left of it to continue the war.[11] Grant's style of warfare, with no fear and with constant pressure all along the line, proved successful. Lee surrendered to Grant at Appomattox Court House, Virginia, on April 9, 1865, bringing an end to much of the fighting and eventual victory for the Federals in the Civil War.

Grant could easily have taken advantage of his successful warfare to have the Confederates pay a hard price for beginning the war and then losing it. Instead Grant instituted a generous peace. He told Lee at Appomattox Court House in April 1865 that "each officer and man will be allowed to return to their homes, not to be disturbed by United States authority so long as they observe their paroles and the laws in force where they may reside." When there was talk of jailing Confederates, including Lee, Grant refused to go along. He had promised Lee to let him go, so no treason charges would be enforced.[12]

So what was the early lesson that propelled Grant to victory in spite of all the obstacles he faced—what did he learn that day in Missouri in 1861 that allowed him to keep pushing forward? He recorded that insight in his memoirs:

> When we reached a point from which the valley below was in full view I halted. The place where Harris had been encamped a few days before was still there and the marks of a recent encampment were plainly visible, but the troops were gone. My heart resumed its place. It occurred to me at once that Harris had been as much afraid of me as I had been of him. This was a view of the question I had never taken before; but it was one I never forgot afterwards. From that event to the close of the war, I never experienced trepidation upon confronting an enemy, though I always felt more or less anxiety. I never forgot that he had as much reason to fear my forces as I had his. The lesson was valuable.[13]

This realization that his opponents feared him as much as he feared them freed Grant to keep pressing forward for the rest of the war, no matter the obstacles. It made him a successful general.

BIRTH-PLACE OF LIEUT.-GEN. U. S. GRANT,
POINT PLEASANT, CLERMONT COUNTY, OHIO.

Ulysses S. Grant's birthplace home in Point Pleasant, Ohio.

General Ulysses S. Grant alone in uniform.

Abraham Lincoln. Library of Congress, Prints & Photographs Division, LC-USZ62-12380.

An unidentified man holding Ulysses S. Grant's horse, Little Jeff Davis.

Ulysses S. Grant in uniform with his family (from the left: Ellen "Nellie" Grant, Ulysses S. Grant, Jesse Grant, Frederick D. Grant, Julia D. Grant, and Ulysses S. "Buck" Grant Jr.)

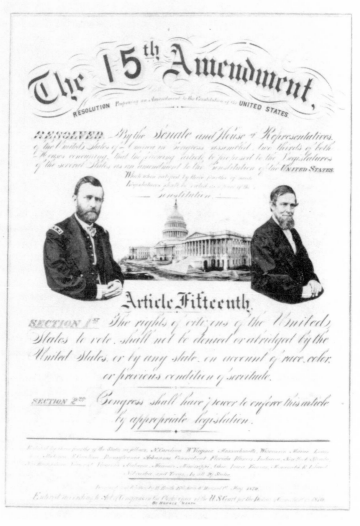

Ulysses S. Grant in uniform with his vice president, Schuyler Colfax, commemorating the passage of the Fifteenth Amendment.

President Ulysses S. Grant.

Ulysses S. Grant (fifth from left), Julia D. Grant (fourth from left), and party at the mines in Virginia City, Nevada, October 28, 1879.

Grant Cottage in Mount McGregor, New York. Ulysses S. Grant passed away in this room on July 23, 1885.

Stephen D. Lee. Courtesy of Special Collections.
Mitchell Memorial Library, Mississippi State University.

SIX

GRANT AND LINCOLN

★ ★ ★ ★

The public criticism was scathing. "All Grant's schemes have failed. He is frittering away time and strength to no purpose. The truth must be told even if it hurts. You cannot make a silk purse out of a sow's ear," wrote Brigadier General Cadwallader C. Washburn during the Vicksburg Campaign. Abraham Lincoln heard such criticism of Grant throughout the war, even in his own home. "He is a butcher," said Mary Todd Lincoln, "and is not fit to be at the head of an army." Lincoln replied, "But he has been very successful in the field." His wife supposedly replied, "Yes, he generally manages to claim a victory, but such a victory! He loses two men to the enemy's one. He has no management, no regard for life."[1] Like his wife, many people tried to influence Lincoln's perceptions of Grant, but what was the actual nature of their relationship?

When the Civil War began, President Lincoln granted numerous military commissions to public figures who were connected politically, thus helping the government to maintain public support for the war. There were, however, trade-offs with this approach. Instead of having experienced military leaders, the Union army was full of novice generals who had to essentially learn on the job, which created an ineffective military force. Even when those men exhibited their lack of experience, they were not removed for fear of alienating key political allies. As a result, the Civil War dragged on and the fighting stalled.[2]

While the political generals stumbled, a lower-ranking general, Ulysses S. Grant, was finding success. He won victories in the Western Theater of the war, the area between the Appalachian Mountains and the Mississippi River, at Forts Henry and Donelson, Shiloh, and Vicksburg. Even with this success, Grant received criticism from military and political leaders all too eager to spread rumors about his alleged drinking. Nonetheless, Lincoln's trust in Grant began to solidify. Lincoln's standard reply to accusations of Grant's alleged drinking was "I can't spare this man—he fights."[3]

After Grant secured a major Union victory in Chattanooga, Tennessee, he was promoted to lieutenant general, making him the first person since George Washington to hold that title. Grant went to Washington to receive his commission in March 1864. This was the first time that Grant and Lincoln met in person, and it appeared their personalities complemented one another. Once Grant took over command of the entire Union army, the questions were obvious: Could he win in the East where other commanding generals had failed? Could Lincoln and Grant forge a partnership that could bring an end to the war?[4]

Grant also supported Lincoln's effort to incorporate free African Americans into the United States Colored Troops as promised in the Emancipation Proclamation of January 1863. Approximately two hundred thousand African Americans served in the Union army during the war. Lincoln found in Grant and his key subordinates a group of generals who would utilize every resource possible, including black troops, in order to get the job done. The president stayed up to date on the latest news from the battlefield, but he provided Grant with the freedom to execute his military strategy.[5]

Before Grant came along, Lincoln usually displayed better strategic insight than most of his commanders. But Lincoln had always been willing to yield strategic power to any general who demonstrated an ability to accomplish the job. By 1864 he was certain that he had found that person—Ulysses S. Grant. Lincoln worked with his commanding general in the establishment of the modern American command system: a commander in chief to establish overall strategy, a general in chief to implement these plans, and a chief of staff to relay appropriate information to everyone.

Utilizing this new and clearly modern military system which Lincoln, with Grant's help, established, the Union army was finally making forward movements in Virginia. Grant stayed with the Army of the Potomac but he left George Meade in direct control. Henry W. Halleck now became chief of staff. He was the tie between Lincoln and Grant and between Grant and his generals.[6] Moreover, Grant and Lincoln both had the ability to see the war in strategic terms. Grant recognized that he had to accept Lincoln's ideas and fight the war on an all-out basis. As Lincoln insisted he do, Grant hit the enemy everywhere at the same time. Lincoln had so much trust in Grant that he recognized that he and his commanding generals were in agreement on how the war should be fought. Consequently, he gave his general a great deal of leeway.

As the Overland Campaign through Virginia commenced, Lincoln and Grant quickly developed a working relationship based on a mutual understanding of the desired goal—to end the war. Lincoln supported Grant's desire to pursue Lee's Army of Northern Virginia wherever it went. In his first one-on-one interview with Grant, Lincoln laid out his expectations. He wanted Grant to "take the responsibility and act, and call on him for all the assistance needed."[7] Grant accepted this duty without any argument. Based on his later writings, it was clear that Grant had intense respect for Lincoln and his ability to handle difficult situations. In his memoirs, Grant stated that he was not a "Lincoln man" before the war, but he did notice his "great ability." He observed that Lincoln "gained influence over men by making them feel that it was a pleasure to serve him" and that he was "not timid, and he was willing to trust his generals in making and executing their plans."[8]

At the Battle of Spotsylvania Court House in May 1864, the Union army lost eleven generals and nearly twenty thousand troops. After the battle, Grant wrote to Secretary of War Edwin M. Stanton in order to reassure him—and Lincoln—of his strategy, "[I] propose to fight it out on this line if it takes me all summer." Lincoln responded, "I have seen your dispatch expressing your unwillingness to break your hold where you are. . . . Hold on with a bulldog grip, and chew and choke as much as possible." He was encouraged by Grant's determination and willingness to attack the enemy, unlike his previous commanding generals.[9]

Although Lincoln had faith in Grant as a military leader, he insisted that his administration handle all peace negotiations. In response to an offer for a military conference with Grant by Confederate General Robert E. Lee on March 2, 1865, Lincoln, through Stanton, instructed Grant to "have no conference with General Lee, unless it be for the capitulation of General Lee's army or on some minor and purely military matter. He [Lincoln] instructs me to say that you are not to decide, discuss, or confer upon any political question." Grant abided by this command. He responded to Lee, "I would state, that I have no authority to accede to your proposition for a conference on the subject proposed. Such authority is vested in the President of the United States alone." This anecdote alone sheds light on how much Grant respected Lincoln's authority and supported his ability to handle the political and diplomatic aspects of the war.[10]

Grant was also adept at the art of diplomacy, which was evident by his handling of the Confederate peace commissioners sent by Confederate President Jefferson Davis to meet with President Lincoln in January 1865. This group was composed of Confederate Vice-President Alexander Stephens, Assistant Confederate Secretary of War John A. Campbell, and Confederate Senator R. M. T. Hunter. Their goal was to end the war as quickly as possible so that the Confederacy could maintain some level of independence and autonomy. Grant was instructed to keep the commissioners with him at City Point, Virginia, because Lincoln and Secretary of War Edwin Stanton were concerned that the optics of meeting with a peace commission would subvert their attempt at ending slavery through the potential passage of the Thirteenth Amendment. They were also worried that the meeting would allow the Confederacy to establish itself as an independent country. Grant made sure that the commission was treated with respect, but he also stayed true to Lincoln's wish of not sending them to meet with the administration immediately. Eventually, the group met with Lincoln in Virginia on February 2, a day after the resolution for the Thirteenth Amendment was approved by Congress and signed by Lincoln. The commissioners were not happy with the results of the meeting, but Grant had done his job.[11]

In spite of all the criticism Lincoln heard about Grant, the two men developed a friendship characterized by mutual respect. An example of the admiration the two men held for one another occurred on the morning of March 29, 1865, as Lincoln returned to Washington after meeting with Grant, General William T. Sherman, and Admiral David D. Porter aboard the *River Queen*. Accounts of the time indicate that Lincoln appeared to be physically and mentally exhausted, but he shook hands with Grant and each of the staff officers present to see him off. Grant and the Union officers with him doffed their hats in deference to the president as his train started from the station, and Lincoln saluted them in return. "Good-by gentlemen," he cried out to them. "God bless you all! Remember, your success is my success."[12] This success would finally come to fruition when Lee surrendered his army at Appomattox Court House, Virginia, on April 9.

Despite the opinions of others and the inevitable setbacks they faced while trying to win a war, Lincoln and Grant worked together well. They respected one another, they learned from their mistakes, and they produced victory. In Grant, Lincoln had finally found a general who understood his vision for ending the war. In fact, it was Lincoln, with little military knowledge, and the stoic Grant, once considered a failure, who led the fight to save the Union.

SEVEN

LET US HAVE PEACE

★ ★ ★ ★

For many Americans, any mention of the civil rights movement brings to mind images from such events as the landmark case of *Brown v. Board of Education* and the Montgomery bus boycott, among many others. These moments highlighted the terrible realities of daily life for African Americans living in a segregated United States. The civil rights movement against segregation in the 1950s and 1960s eventually succeeded in overturning the racist laws that established those social structures. However, there was an even earlier time when politicians worked to overhaul the legal system, and African American citizens successfully protested segregation laws. For example, streetcars in New Orleans, Louisiana, became integrated in the spring of 1867 after weeks of protest.[1] But this raises further questions: How did those nineteenth-century steps toward integration begin? And how were they rolled back and replaced with a segregated society that lasted well past the middle of the twentieth century?

The answers to these questions lie in the turbulent period that followed the Civil War. What should have been a joyous ending to the Civil War was overshadowed by the assassination of Abraham Lincoln in 1865. Grant had enjoyed a pleasant and productive working relationship with Lincoln, but his relationship with the new president, Andrew Johnson, was just the opposite. Grant served as the commanding general and even, briefly, as interim secretary of war, but he and Johnson remained opposed to one another. Johnson was impeached and almost removed from office in February 1868, setting the stage for Grant's eventual nomination. As one of the nation's most recognizable Civil War heroes, Grant was even more popular than the late Abraham Lincoln. Grant never wanted to run for the presidency, but he felt he had to. He worried, after his experience with Johnson, that the nation would not preserve the victory just achieved and would allow the nation to slide back into prewar chaos.[2]

The years 1863–1877, encompassing the presidential administrations of Abraham Lincoln, Andrew Johnson, and Ulysses S. Grant, have become known as Reconstruction. The main conflicts of the era centered on questions of the role of former slaves. Optimistic plans for postwar economic growth and prosperity in the South quickly evaporated, with African Americans particularly impoverished. Yet in the early years of Reconstruction, previously marginalized groups like African American men and poor whites had the opportunity to vote, to hold office, to serve on juries, and to enjoy a variety of society's benefits that they had never had the opportunity to experience before.[3]

The former ruling class, feeling left out, quickly organized to restore the old system of life, based on white supremacy and black inferiority. They labeled the new governments that included black representation as corrupt and degraded. The old white leadership determined to overthrow the new democratic Southern governments and restore their control. They wanted to make sure that the former slaves remained relegated to the role that they had been forced into for years—that of cheap labor. White Southerners used systematic terror through the Ku Klux Klan to enforce their agenda. Meanwhile, the federal government also made severe cuts to the army, leaving insufficient troops to enforce protection for black rights in the former Confederate states.[4]

Ulysses S. Grant's presidency lasted from 1869 to 1877, the majority of the Reconstruction era. He oversaw a reunited nation whose white citizens—both Northern and Southern—questioned whether blacks could ever be included as full citizens. With indifference or hostility in the North to the plight of newly freed African Americans, white Southerners sought to re-create a form of the prewar Southern society as if the Confederates had actually won the Civil War. "There has never been a moment since Lee surrendered," Grant said, "that I would not have gone more than halfway to meet the Southern people in a spirit of conciliation. But they have never responded to it. They have not forgotten the war."[5]

Yet the period of Reconstruction saw much progress on equality at the federal level with important amendments being successfully added to the Constitution—the Thirteenth outlawed "involuntary servitude," and the Fourteenth declared that every person born in the United States was a citizen with equal protection and due process. With Congressional approval of the Fifteenth Amendment in February 1869, the government could no longer bar citizens from voting based on race.[6]

The ratification of the Fifteenth Amendment on March 30, 1870, extended voting rights to African American men and prompted Grant to take unprecedented action. He sent a special message to Congress that same day, something that a president did not have to do. Grant wrote that the Fifteenth

Amendment was "a measure of grander importance than any other one act of the kind from the foundation of our free Government to the present day." Echoing Lincoln's sentiments, Grant proclaimed, "To the race more favored heretofore by our laws I would say, Withhold no legal privilege of advancement to the new citizen." He wrote, "I repeat that the adoption of the fifteenth amendment to the Constitution completes the greatest civil change, and constitutes the most important event that has occurred, since the nation came into life."[7]

Grant was so pleased with the ratification of the Fifteenth Amendment because it allowed the passage of the Enforcement Act in 1870 that gave federal authorities the power to suppress the activities of the notorious Ku Klux Klan. Including members from all elements of Southern society and led by the traditional white leadership, the Klan prevented blacks from voting and tried to destroy the Republican Party in the South by murdering its black and white leaders. Local groups of Klansmen carried out a widespread campaign of violence across the South against blacks and whites who supported African American civil rights. In one such case in Alabama in 1870, Irish-born teacher William Luke and four black men were lynched. The Klan also carried out violence against women as well as men.[8]

Faced with the horrors of such brutal crimes, Grant responded. He went to the Congress in 1871 and received authorization to use the military to combat all white supremacist groups. He was also authorized to suspend habeas corpus to facilitate jailing suspected Klan members. His vision was for African Americans to become full citizens of the United States. Under a newly created Department of Justice, federal marshals working with US troops arrested suspected Klansmen across the South. The Grant administration then dealt a crippling blow to the Klan, trying, convicting, and jailing many of the terror group's leaders and bringing relative peace to the South.[9]

But then the progress of Reconstruction stalled. Although Grant had successfully dealt with the initial threat posed by the KKK, many in the North did not favor continued involvement in the ongoing conflicts in the South. Thaddeus Stevens, a leader of the Radical Republican effort, had died, and other Republicans who had little interest in African American civil rights rose to prominent positions in the party. The Northern public became tired of federal intervention in the South and believed that enough had been done to set the stage for African American postwar success. On top of all this, the economic depression of 1873 became the focus of national politicians, no matter what Grant's Reconstruction policies sought to achieve.[10]

Grant's 1870–71 successful stand against the Ku Klux Klan's attempt to thwart civil rights and equality eventually gave way to Jim Crow laws and nearly a hundred years of legalized segregation. This happened despite the dictates of the Civil War amendments and the Civil Rights Acts of 1866 and 1875. Support in the North for Reconstruction policies cooled, and Democrats won control of the House of Representatives in the elections of 1874. At the same time, legal challenges to the newly adopted civil rights amendments gained traction in the courts and allowed states significant leeway in how they could curb African American civil rights. Despite Grant's continued popularity and his personal convictions, the gains of Reconstruction were being systematically rolled back.[11]

As Northern support for Reconstruction faded, violence again erupted across the South, and the federal government could do little to curb it. The bitter irony was that without the willing support of so many of their wartime enemies, the former Confederates would not have been able to achieve what they did in dismantling the reforms of Reconstruction. As the Civil War receded further into the past, many in the North had had enough. For them the meaning of Grant's famous election slogan, "Let us have peace," was pulling away from Reconstruction.[12]

One critique of Grant's view of Reconstruction is that he may not have realized that changing the South from its slavery-based society to a civic sphere of free people would require a true revolution and not just legislative and social reform. The conflict during Andrew Johnson's presidency only compounded the nation's troubles, and Grant was forced to juggle an unbelievable domestic agenda—not only in the context of continuing strife in the South but also from the scandals initiated by his own friends whom he had trusted. Yet he tried to uphold Lincoln's vision of maintaining an open society with justice for all.

Like the African Americans who demanded integrated streetcars in New Orleans, President Ulysses S. Grant was far ahead of his time in believing in and pushing for racial equality. But during Reconstruction and the years that followed, no American who believed that African Americans and white Americans should share in the fruits of togetherness could ever be seen as great or even adequate in the presidency. State politicians eventually reinstated a form of segregation in the streetcars of New Orleans in 1902.[13] Likewise, Grant's belief in equality doomed his reputation.

It took the social and racial reforms of the 1960s to demonstrate why Grant's belief in racial equality during his presidency would hurt his historical reputation—a reputation that is changing today in light of the modern civil rights movement.

EIGHT

GILDED AGE CORRUPTION

★ ★ ★ ★

In February of 1876 a courtroom in St. Louis, Missouri, was the scene of a drama that seemed to heighten in intensity with each passing day. President Ulysses S. Grant's private secretary, Orville Babcock, stood accused of being involved with what was dubbed "The Whiskey Ring," a group of conspirators who siphoned off federal tax money for their own personal gain. The spectacle of the trial and the closeness of the accused to the president himself captured the public's imagination. There were even reports that Grant would appear at the trial and perhaps even testify in support of Babcock.[1] The questions lingered: what would Grant do, and would the trial reveal that Grant himself was involved?

Grant was elected to the presidency in 1868, taking office in March of 1869. He faced a daunting domestic agenda as he took office. The terrible conflict of the Civil War had ended in 1865, but then President Abraham Lincoln had been assassinated just a few days afterwards, and his assassination had resulted in the tumultuous presidency of Andrew Johnson. The Tennessean's time in office was marked by conflict over African American rights and the process for bringing the former Confederate states back into the Union. Eventually in 1868 Johnson's opponents in Congress impeached him, and he avoided formal removal from office by only one vote. Although he survived the impeachment process, he did not receive the 1868 nomination as the Democratic candidate for President.[2]

In this painfully divided atmosphere, Americans looked to Ulysses S. Grant as a logical candidate to bring the nation together. He was admired by those in the North for his leadership of the Union army during the Civil War and was well regarded by those in the South for his generous terms of surrender and emphasis on reconciliation. He did not actively campaign for the Republican nomination, but accepted it in a letter that included his famous statement "Let us have peace."[3]

Many Americans viewed Grant's victory in the 1868 presidential election as a note of hope for the beleaguered nation,[4] but Southern whites continued to resist federal efforts to secure African American rights. Grant began his presidency committed to guarantee newly freed African Americans their full rights as citizens of the nation in spite of violence by the Ku Klux Klan.[5]

As if these daunting challenges were not enough, the Grant administration faced a host of other issues stemming from the rapid development of the post–Civil War economy and changes in society. The post–Civil War era came to be known as the Gilded Age, taking its name from the title of an 1873 novel by Mark Twain and Charles Dudley Warner. In this novel a thin coating of gold covered over a mass of ugliness underneath. Later scholars and social commentators applied the term to that era of the late nineteenth century because great wealth and prosperity characterized the lives of some, while most others suffered from dire poverty.[6]

During this era, a common public belief was that government, at all levels, was corrupt. Carrying out the war effort in the 1860s had involved large expenditures from public coffers, and the distribution of that money meant that it passed through a large bureaucracy. The reality of corrupt military and civilian officials siphoning off funds illegally and the fear that theft and embezzlement were rampant fueled the public's concerns that corruption was entrenched in all levels of government.[7]

In addition, many Americans were suspicious of almost any governmental spending for public projects, worrying that these projects were unnecessary expenditures that only rewarded constituents in certain districts for their support of particular candidates. These types of projects are often characterized in modern American politics as being "pork barrel," and there was no shortage of these same criticisms during the Gilded Age.[8]

Finally, the system of political patronage in operation at the time further eroded public confidence in the government. Prior to the passage of meaningful civil service reform legislation in the 1880s, it was common practice for elected politicians to reward their supporters not just with pork barrel projects but with jobs in government. These jobs provided income and influence and functioned as powerful incentives to support certain candidates.[9] The general public read news of the scandals, resulting from illegal and ethically questionable practices, and viewed all governmental activity with a skeptical eye.[10]

Grant's presidency, on top of all the other challenges it faced, was not immune to suspicion. Both the dominant Republican Party and the Democrats leveled charges of corruption against Grant during his presidency. As a way to oppose Grant's civil rights activities, Democrats insisted that Grant's administration was corrupt. Some Republicans, like

Charles Sumner, likewise looked down on Grant because he was not a New England intellectual like they were.[11]

In this climate, even the president himself was suspected of wrongdoing, as in the case of the Gold Ring of 1869. Businessmen Jay Gould and James Fisk befriended Grant's brother-in-law Abel Corbin and used that connection to become acquainted with Grant. They then leveraged this acquaintance to try to influence US Treasury policy. They tried to convince Grant to limit the Treasury's sale of gold and thus drive up the price. When Grant discovered their scheme in September 1869, he took measures to lower the price of gold, thereby undermining their attempt. Grant's response prevented a major economic depression but created short-term disruptions in the economy. The speculators' connections to the president and his own brother-in-law added to the perception of corruption in the economy and at all levels of government. In fact, Grant himself was cleared of any wrongdoing by a subsequent congressional investigation.[12]

The early 1870s also saw the rise of accusations of widespread corruption by those overseeing the New York customhouse. These alleged activities drew the attention of the Senate Committee on Investigation and Retrenchment, a committee established by Grant's political opponents to investigate his actions as president. Officials in the New York customhouse oversaw import and export traffic for one of the busiest ports in the United States, and accusations surfaced that Grant-appointed customs collectors, including Moses H. Grinnell and Thomas Murphy, had conspired with George K. Leet, a former military staffer of Grant's during the Civil War, to allow him to secure more and more control over the business of storing imported goods. Leet was thus able to increase his fees (and therefore his revenues), frustrating merchants who had to deal with the higher costs. Although the public was captivated by accusations of a "Custom House Ring," the Senate investigation found that many abuses of the system alleged in the press had not occurred at all. The practices that had been deemed questionable had already been changed by Chester A. Arthur, the newly appointed collector and future president of the United States. Nonetheless, the accusation of corrupt practices by public officials appointed by Grant further influenced public perception.[13]

While accusations against the practices of low-level presidential appointees certainly created problems, accusations of inappropriate actions by cabinet members carried far more weight and resulted in even wider-ranging consequences. In 1875 Secretary of the Interior Columbus Delano resigned after accusations arose that he had tolerated improper practices in his department. Under Delano's watch, the Department of the Interior had awarded government contracts to his son, John, and President Grant's brother, Orvil, both of whom were unqualified for the work and never completed it.[14] Delano's successor, Zachariah Chandler, was instructed by Grant to clean up the department, and these efforts uncovered additional corrupt practices. So while many of his reforms were successful, the airing of more dirty laundry and the implication of the president's own brother in the scandal resulted in more suspicion from taxpayers about what government officials were actually doing.[15]

In February of 1876 testimony during an investigation by members of the House of Representatives revealed a scheme involving yet another cabinet member. Beginning in 1870, Secretary of War William Belknap had persuaded Congress to allow the War Department to award contracts for trading posts at forts in the western United States. Native Americans did extensive business at those trading posts, and the individuals, mostly non–Native Americans, who were awarded contracts stood to make significant profits. In exchange for maintaining his post contract, John S. Evans provided Carrie Belknap, wife of the secretary of war, payments based on the profits from the operation of the trading post at Fort Sill, Oklahoma. After Carrie Belknap's death, her husband and his third wife continued to accept such payments. When the arrangement was revealed, Belknap approached Grant at the White House on March 2, 1876, in a panic and offered his resignation. Grant had just learned that the investigation had implicated Belknap, but he did not yet have the full information. Nonetheless, he accepted Belknap's resignation. This move was widely criticized because it shielded Belknap from prosecution as he was no longer a government employee.[16]

The most infamous of the scandals that occurred during the Grant administration came the closest to touching Grant himself. The so-called Whiskey Ring involved distillers bribing government officials to mark untaxed barrels of whiskey as taxed, thus defrauding the government of significant revenue.[17]

The scheme was most prominent in St. Louis, Missouri, but the network of corrupt officials extended well beyond that city. It eventually involved distillers, distributors, and government officials in Chicago, Milwaukee, and numerous other cities. In May 1875 United States Secretary of the Treasury Benjamin Bristow discovered the fraud and indicted hundreds of conspirators throughout the country, uncovering evidence of over four million dollars in stolen tax revenue, which is worth approximately ninety million dollars in modern money.[18]

One of the most newsworthy results of Bristow's investigation was the indictment of Orville Babcock, Grant's long-time friend and military aide who also served as his private secretary during his presidency. In December 1875 Babcock was charged with tax fraud and conspiracy. He denied any wrongdoing and went on trial in St. Louis.[19] During the trial, Babcock was accused of using his prominent position in the Grant White House to provide information to other members of the Whiskey Ring about the progress of the investigation.[20]

Grant believed in Babcock, proclaiming that he was as "confident as he lived" that his friend was innocent.[21] He even considered testifying at the trial on Babcock's behalf, because he was so convinced that the accusations against his friend were nothing more than politically motivated attempts to slander his presidency. However, the members of Grant's cabinet objected to the idea of a sitting president testifying during a trial.[22] So on February 12, 1876, Grant gave a deposition at the White House in which he affirmed his confidence in Babcock. The *New York Times* summarized his statement this way: "if Gen. Babcock had been engaged in any wrong transactions the President had no knowledge of it, and he did not believe it."[23]

Grant's deposition coupled with a lack of concrete evidence against Babcock resulted in his acquittal in February 1876.[24] Many modern scholars believe that Babcock was most likely guilty, but that Grant's deposition helped him escape prosecution. Soon after the trial Grant learned that his friend had been involved in the Gold Ring in 1869. This shook Grant's trust in Babcock, and Grant's old friend never regained his influential position in the administration.[25]

Unfortunately, the damage had been done. Grant himself was never shown to have been personally involved in the scandals that occurred during his presidency, yet the aura of scandal and the political turmoil that the nation experienced during the Gilded Age remained as a symbol of that era. In the popular imagination, the Whiskey Ring and all the other scandals during Grant's presidency gave rise to the enduring impression of Grant as bogged down by corruption. The evidence, instead, points to a nation suffering through the traumatic aftermath of the Civil War and a president who remained loyal to his friends. Grant did his best to steer the nation through turbulent and chaotic times swirling around him, in spite of friends who too often let him down.

NINE

TOURING THE WORLD

★ ★ ★ ★

In 1877 Lieutenant Commander Albert G. Caldwell, an officer on the ship USS *Vandalia*, bemoaned the presence of one of his esteemed passengers. He wrote, "We are to take the great ring-master about the Mediterranean, it has cost me much annoyance and trouble already—I hope we will get heavy gale on his first visit and then he will leave for good."[1] Caldwell was talking about former president Ulysses S. Grant, who, along with his wife, Julia, and son Jesse, was taking a trip around the world, the first of its kind by any sitting or former president. But if Grant's own countryman was underwhelmed by his presence, what impact, if any, would he have on people of other nations?

In early 1877, as he came to the end of his two terms as president, Grant determined to take a trip around the world. In a letter to John F. Long, the man who maintained the Grant family's St. Louis property while they were away, Grant indicated that he had no specific plans about where he, Julia, and Jesse would travel or how long they would be gone. But he estimated that they would not return "until the party becomes homesick which may be in six months, and may not be for two years."[2] Unbeknownst to Grant, his trip to Europe would morph from his plan of recreation into the first postpresidential diplomatic world tour. From May 1877 until December 1879 Grant met with foreign dignitaries, famous artists, writers, and explorers. He visited historic sites and even acted as a mediator between Japan and China in order to quell hostilities between the two countries.

Before Grant could make any official plans to travel to Europe, he needed to find a way to fund the trip. He used the money he had acquired by investing the gifts he had received after the Civil War. The only expense that he did not pay for on this trip was the use of the many navy ships that would take him and his family around the globe; the United States government paid those costs.

The presidential election of 1876 created domestic intrigue prior to Grant's world tour but ended with a president in office who saw potential in Grant's travels. Rutherford B. Hayes, the Republican governor of Ohio, had lost the popular vote to Democratic governor Samuel J. Tilden of New York, but there was a long, drawn-out dispute over who had won the Electoral College. Hayes ended up winning the election in controversial fashion, and on February 20, 1877, Grant invited him and his family to dinner at the White House. It is unclear just what the two political leaders talked about specifically, but the fellow Republicans enjoyed a cordial relationship based on their previous conversations on political matters. As the Grants left the US, the Hayes administration instructed all American diplomats abroad to be on the lookout for ways to welcome and assist the Grant family in their travels. In addition, Secretary of the Navy Richard Thompson offered the services of US Navy vessels to the Grants. These gestures indicate the opportunity that the Hayes administration saw in Grant's travels to further US interests overseas.[3]

After Grant left the White House on March 5, he and
Julia stayed three weeks at the home of his secretary of state,
Hamilton Fish. Their plans were to travel west so they could
visit with family and friends and make arrangements for
their properties before embarking on their world tour. They
visited St. Louis, Chicago, Galena, and Cincinnati before
returning to the East to visit with family and friends in New-
ark, Elizabeth, and Morristown, New Jersey.[4]

On May 9 Grant attended the opening of an exhibit for
the Centennial Exposition in Philadelphia, Pennsylvania. He
made plans to start the world tour soon after their visit to
Philadelphia, but his son Jesse was slow to join his parents
there. In a moment of frustration, Grant scolded his son. He
stated, "You young worthless ... You know we sail on the 17th
and if you should not be here you will be left without visible
means of support. I shall make no arrangement for you in
our absence."[5] Jesse did not take his father's threat lightly. He
caught up with his parents just in time. The trio, along with
a few servants, departed on May 17 for England aboard USS
Indiana, and they arrived to a cheering crowd in Liverpool
on May 28.

Over the next month, Grant traveled around the London
area meeting with poets, novelists, playwrights, and the royal
family. In London, too, they met with old friends Edwards
Pierrepont and family, who introduced them to members of
the royal family. Their first dinner in London was with the
Duke of Wellington and, as Julia put it, "England's noblest
men and women."[6] On June 18 Grant attended breakfast
with three of England's well-known writers: Anthony Trol-
lope, Robert Browning, and Matthew Arnold. As a lover of
fiction, Grant certainly enjoyed meeting these literary giants.
A few days later, on June 23, Grant had the pleasure of dining

with the Prince of Wales (and the future king of England), Albert Edward. Soon after, the Grants made a visit to War-sash, where their daughter Nellie resided with her English husband and his family.

Perhaps the highlight of Grant's visit to England was his meeting with Queen Victoria. After receiving an invitation to dine with the queen, the Grants, along with United States consul general to London, Adam Badeau, arrived at Wind-sor Castle on June 26. When they arrived, they were given a brief tour of the castle's artwork and shown to their room. Soon after, the Grant party met with the queen outside of her private apartment. A dinner was to be held at a private table where only the most notable people sat. However, a point of contention soon developed. Jesse and Badeau were informed that they would not be sitting at the queen's table but instead would be dining with the queen's household— her most honored attendants. Jesse responded that he would rather return to London than sit with "the servants." Ulysses immediately inquired about Jesse's place at the table, and the queen responded by saying that she "would be happy to have Mr. Jesse dine at her table." The dinner did not last long, but the queen made sure to speak to every guest, including Jesse. The Grants were well received by the royal family, but some people, specifically the Earl of Derby, later labeled Ulysses as "the roughest specimen we had yet had from the west" and compared his intelligence and manners to that of a "bull-dog." The queen was impressed by Julia's civility and man-ners, but she was not as dazzled by Jesse, whom she called "a very ill-mannered young Yankee."[7]

The Grants then made their way to the mainland of Europe on July 5, where they met with King Leopold of Belgium in Brussels. From there, the Grant party traveled quickly throughout the rest of the continent. They visited Germany, where they met famed composer Richard Wagner, and Switzerland and northern Italy before making their way back to England. While in England for the second time, they toured Scotland and visited with their daughter Nellie again, and Ulysses spoke in Birmingham where he had the chance to meet businessman and statesman Joseph Chamberlain. The next phase of their journey took the family to Paris. Grant had an opportunity to see the construction of a gift the French were planning on giving the United States, the Statue of Liberty. Even though the French were gracious to him, Grant was not impressed by their capital. He said, "I have seen nothing here that would make me want to live in Paris."[8]

From France the Grants traveled aboard USS *Vandalia* to Alexandria, Egypt. On their way they stopped at the historical cities of Genoa and Naples, Italy, where they visited Pompeii and had the opportunity to ascend Mount Vesuvius. Their party arrived at Alexandria on January 5, 1878. While there, Grant met with Welsh journalist and explorer, Henry M. Stanley, who had participated in the American Civil War. The following two weeks were spent traveling the Nile River by steamer. After exploring the ruins at Thebes and Memphis, the party made its way to the Holy Land. From the end of February until the end of March, they visited Turkey, Constantinople, and Greece. On March 18 they arrived back in Naples.

During his second trip to Naples, Grant had the opportunity to meet Pope Leo XIII. Before visiting the pope, however, he was compelled to meet with the newly anointed King Umberto of Italy. This demand demonstrated the complicated relationship between church and state in Italy at the time. The meeting between Ulysses and the Pope was cordial. The two conversed in French with Jesse translating for his father. After meeting with the Pope, the party traveled to Florence, Venice, Milan, Turin, and Dijon. On May 9 they returned to Paris to see the Paris Universal Exposition, but Grant was once again unimpressed. On June 14 the party traveled throughout Holland. They visited The Hague, Rotterdam, and Amsterdam. Ulysses was thoroughly impressed by what he saw in the Netherlands. He called it "the most interesting country—and people—that I have yet seen."[9]

The next stop on Grant's trip was to visit Berlin where he met one of his greatest admirers, Chancellor Otto von Bismarck. Grant was familiar with Bismarck and his ability to maintain relative order in his country during a time of civil unrest because Philip Sheridan, whom Grant had sent to observe the Franco-Prussian War, had prepped him. On June 30 Grant received an invitation to meet with Bismarck and, ignoring a grand entrance, Grant simply walked up to the door and asked to see the chancellor.

The two military leaders had a personal, in-depth discussion about war, politics, and their respective countries. During their meeting, John Russell Young, a journalist who was accompanying Grant on his world tour, made note of what was discussed between the two military leaders. Perhaps the most notable part of the discussion dealt with the American Civil War. Bismarck remarked, "What always seemed so sad to me about your last great war was that you were fighting your own people. That is always so terrible in wars, so very hard." Grant replied succinctly that "It had to be done." To which Bismarck responded, "Yes, you had to save the Union just as we had to save Germany." Grant then responded, "Not only to save the Union, but destroy slavery." Bismarck pushed back, "I suppose, however, the Union was the real sentiment, the dominant sentiment." Grant reiterated his point, "In the beginning, yes, but as soon as slavery fired upon the flag it was felt, we all felt, even those who did not object to slaves, that slavery must be destroyed. We felt that it was a stain to the Union that men should be bought and sold like cattle." After more discussion, Bismarck walked Grant to the door, the two shook hands, Grant lit a cigar, and he left the palace.[10]

After his cordial meeting with Bismarck, Grant continued on his tour. He visited Copenhagen, toured Scandinavia, and traveled to Warsaw, St. Petersburg, and Moscow, where he met with Tsar Alexander II. He also met with Emperor Franz Joseph I in Vienna, explored the Alps, and met with German Emperor Wilhelm I near Salzburg. In October Grant met with the king of Spain and visited numerous cities throughout the country.[11] In January 1879, before the Grant family left for Asia, Grant's eldest son Fred joined them. Then they boarded a French steamer on their way east. At this point in the trip, Grant began to keep a journal which provided great insight into his experience. Once they arrived at the Suez Canal, they boarded a British vessel headed for Bombay, India. While there, the group visited the Taj Mahal, rode elephants, toured schools, and explored ancient ruins near Delhi.

In March Grant met with Viceroy Edward Robert Bulwer-Lytton, a fiction writer who later wrote a wild, unflattering, and patently false account of Grant's visit. From India the group made their way through Singapore, Bangkok, Saigon, and into China. While in China, they visited Shanghai, Peking, the Great Wall of China, and the Temple of Heaven. Grant was not impressed by the historic temple. In his journal he stated that it was "not worth the trouble of a visit."[12]

Although Grant was clearly enjoying himself as a tourist, he could not escape the diplomatic duties foreign dignitaries placed upon him. While meeting with Prince Kung, an important statesman in China, Grant agreed to act as a mediator between China and Japan over a dispute regarding the Ryukyu Islands, which are a string of islands situated on the boundary of the East China Sea and the Philippine Sea between Japan and Taiwan. Within two weeks the Grant party had traveled to Japan. They visited Nagasaki and Tokyo. On July 4, 1879, Grant himself met with Emperor Meiji and Empress Shōken. A little over a month later, Grant wrote a letter to both the Chinese and Japanese governments in hopes of establishing a conference between the two countries that would settle the dispute over the islands, one of which was today's Okinawa.[13] To Grant's dismay, the talks later fell apart, and the dispute was never officially settled. Soon after, despite China's objections, Japan annexed the islands.[14]

On September 3 the Grant party left Japan aboard the ship *City of Tokio* and headed back to America. They made a stop in San Francisco, California, before visiting Vancouver in the Washington Territory where Grant had been stationed after fighting in the Mexican-American War. They explored the Yosemite Valley, Nevada, the Utah Territory, and the Wyoming Territory, among other places throughout the heart of the continent. After roughly two years the tour ended when they arrived back in Philadelphia on December 16. Ten days later, on December 26, Grant met privately with President Hayes and more than likely updated him on all he had seen and done.

Grant's world tour was a grand experience, but considering his status on the world stage at that time, this trip was historic. It was the first of its kind, and it helped shape the world's opinion not just of Grant but also of the United States itself. The leaders and citizens of the nations he visited viewed him as an emissary of American democracy—an ordinary man who had risen to the nation's highest office by merit rather than noble birth. His travels set the precedent for the work of modern former presidents who serve as goodwill ambassadors for the United States. Grant's unpretentious style charmed many around the world, including Lieutenant Commander Caldwell, the officer on USS *Vandalia,* who set aside his preconceived notions after getting to know the former president. He later wrote, "My opinion of old USG has changed wonderfully—he is as pleasant and jolly as can be and I can see how he had friends who stuck to him through thick and thin."[15]

TEN

A FINAL FAREWELL

★ ★ ★ ★

On July 23, 1885, Ulysses Grant died at Mount McGregor, New York. His family had been left penniless by an unscrupulous business partner, and he had raced against death to finish his memoirs so that his family, especially his beloved wife Julia, would have some kind of income. Charles L. Webster and Company, the publisher of Grant's memoirs, had been optimistic about the sales potential of the book, but the success of any book is never guaranteed. The first royalty check did not even arrive until after Grant's death. Was Grant's widow actually helped financially by the publication of his memoirs?

It all began long before Grant's last years. Former soldiers in the Civil War, on both sides of the conflict, and of all ranks, were publishing articles in *Century Magazine*'s Battles and Leaders series.[1] Some were also preparing book-length memoirs, but Grant had no interest in writing either articles or a book. Whenever anyone suggested that he undertake such a task, he politely said no. He sincerely believed that the public would not be interested in anything he had to say. Besides, he had helped a former military aide, Adam Badeau, research a three-volume history of Grant's Civil War career, so anytime anyone wanted him to write anything, he insisted that it was already "in Badeau."[2]

In fact, had Grant not experienced tragic circumstances which turned his entire life upside-down, he would never have written his memoirs. In 1880 he joined his son Buck and the "Wizard of Wall Street," Ferdinand Ward, in the investment firm of Grant and Ward. Money flowed in and out of the company, and Grant could not have been happier with the results. On May 4, 1884, however, the whole operation collapsed. Ward proved to be a charlatan, operating a scheme where he used the same collateral for multiple loans. When the investments did not pay off, the firm was left without sufficient funds to pay its debts. Grant was suddenly bankrupt even though he took a loan of $150,000 from William H. Vanderbilt, the head of the New York Central Railroad Company, to try to keep Grant and Ward afloat. The only money he had was what he could find in his trouser pockets and his wife's purse. He was determined to pay off the loan, even if it meant giving up all the assets he and Julia had accumulated. He was in the midst of a disaster.[3]

Grant's financial misfortune became public, so the editors of *Century* approached him yet again to write something for their Battles and Leaders series. Grant still hesitated, but now he had no real choice. He needed the money. The magazine offered five hundred dollars an article for four essays: on Shiloh, Vicksburg, the Wilderness, and Chattanooga. He took the offer.

Grant first went to work on an article concerning Shiloh, and the result was terrible: the prose was stiff and boring, really a battle report and not an article. The editors decided that the youngest editor would visit Grant to try to explain to the general just how bad the article was. Robert U. Johnson sat down with Grant at the former general's New Jersey summer home in mid-June 1884 and carefully indicated what

Grant had to do to make the article acceptable. Johnson told Grant to write the way he spoke, so that more of his personality came through. Grant took the advice and rewrote the essay, making it appealing to the ordinary reader. In the process he came to see that he actually enjoyed writing and had something to say.[4] It was a literary breakthrough for him.

Several weeks before this insight, in July 1884, while he was eating lunch with his family, he had suffered another setback. He bit into a peach and immediately felt a sharp pain in the back of his mouth. He thought that perhaps there had been a bee on the peach, and it had stung him. He tried a glass of water, but that only made his throat feel like it was on fire. Day after day, the pain remained, and Julia urged him to see a doctor. He refused. When a physician came to visit a neighbor, he was asked to look at Grant's throat. One look, and he urged Grant to see his family physician. Again, Grant said no. He did not go back to New York until the fall, and even then his doctor was in Europe. It was not until the last days of October 1884, when Grant's family doctor returned from Europe, that he looked into the general's mouth. He immediately sent the ex-president to a famous throat specialist.

Dr. John Hancock Douglas had known Grant since his involvement with the United States Sanitary Commission during the Civil War. He looked into his former general's mouth and must have given some indication of a major problem, because Grant immediately asked, "Is it cancer?" Yes, it was. It was carcinoma of the right tonsillar pillar. And there was nothing that doctors in that age could do to cure it. All that was possible was to ease the pain by having the patient gargle with permanganate, potash, and brewer's yeast. Or doctors might try codeine, morphine, brandy, or a cocaine and water solution. Douglas and other doctors tried everything they could, but it did not make the cancer go away. Grant even had some diseased teeth pulled, in case they were the source of the problem. Nothing worked. His health only grew worse, and Grant became even more miserable.

The prospect of his fatal illness made Grant finally consider taking on a major writing project. Magazine articles would produce five hundred dollars an article, but two thousand dollars would not solve all his financial woes. He began considering something that he never would have thought of before. Perhaps he would write his memoirs in order to make enough money to support his wife and family when he died from the horrible disease afflicting his mouth. The *Century* editors even had a contract ready for him to sign, which he read the very day he had visited Dr. Douglas. Knowing about his cancer, he seemed ready to take the step he had avoided so long: sign a contract to produce his memoirs.[5]

Now entered the individual who was to play a leading role in all that followed: Samuel L. Clemens. The author, more famously known as Mark Twain, was appalled when he learned that *Century* was only going to pay Grant a royalty of 10 percent, the same amount that they would pay an unknown, first-time author who would sell only a few copies of his writings. Twain convinced Grant that he would be making a horrible mistake if he signed with *Century*. Instead, he told Grant to sign with his new business, Charles L. Webster and Company. He would pay him 70 percent of the profit. Grant was pleased with this offer, and although he thought he might still be honor-bound to sign with the magazine company, he decided to accept Twain's offer. Grant would do all the writing, and Twain would take care of the business side.[6]

Grant had already begun writing, but now he pressed forward even more desperately. He knew he was dying from cancer, and he had to complete his writing before he died. He had to leave his wife a sufficient source of income to provide for her after his death. His writing became his obsession, and he wrote feverishly five to seven hours a day, sometimes dictating, other times writing out the text longhand.[7]

At that time Grant was living in New York City on East Sixty-Sixth Street and was doing most of his composing in what he called his library. This room only had one window and one fireplace. He was constantly surrounded by family members and friends. His son Fred helped him check facts, and so did his sons Buck and Jesse. His own memory of the war also helped insure the accuracy of his writing. His aide Adam Badeau was also present, and so was his African American servant Harrison Terrell.[8] His writing seemed to give him the energy to overcome the throat pain. Often he even refused the numbing medicine because it made him feel sleepy and caused him difficulty concentrating.

Julia hovered over him, wishing that there was something she could do to help ease his torment. He was particularly happy when grandchildren came into his room, and he loved seeing his daughters-in-law. But it was the writing that remained his driving force. The street outside his home became clogged with reporters and people hoping to catch a glimpse of him. He wrote as fast as he could. He had to finish before his life was snuffed out and his wife left bankrupt.

Mark Twain visited regularly, although his own travels kept him from being constantly at the general's side. He never attempted to contribute more than a few suggestions because he understood that this was Grant's book. Despite later claims, Twain did not write any of the memoirs. He appreciated

Grant's unique voice. Not known as an astute businessman himself, Twain served as Grant's business manager and financial advisor. Ironically, his financial advice proved better for Grant's memoirs than it did for his own publications.[9]

Grant's work grew increasingly more painful, however. It proved impossible for him to lie flat on his back because the cancer-induced phlegm caused him to feel like he was going to choke. Clearly, the only thing that kept him alive was his writing regimen. He grew sicker, but he refused to stop. He had to complete his book before he died—for Julia and his family's sake.

Working in his New York home, Grant began to suffer further discomfort at the onset of Manhattan's famous summer heat and humidity. He was miserable enough from his cancer, but then the weather made him feel even worse. Fortunately an old friend, philanthropist and civic leader Joseph Drexel, owned a summer cottage on Mount McGregor, near Saratoga Springs, New York, and offered the home for Grant's use that summer. The coolness of the Adirondacks made it logical to move Grant there. The weather had no impact on his cancer, however, but it still felt more comfortable there than it did in the humid city. On June 16, 1885, he was moved, along with his family, a number of friends, and supporters to what today is called the Grant Cottage on Mount McGregor.[10]

Grant knew better than anyone else just how sick he was, and his affection for his beloved Julia only increased as he fought death to complete his memoirs for her benefit. In his illness he worried about what funeral arrangements she would have to make when he died. He knew that he could give her instructions personally, but he did not want to upset her.

Consequently, he chose a method that would cause her the least pain and worry. He wrote her a letter on June 29, 1885, but he did not give it to her directly. In the letter, he said that he had known for a long time that he was dying and that "the end is not far off." So he wanted to tell her that he himself preferred the United States Military Academy for his burial, but since she would not be allowed to be buried next to him there, "I therefore leave you free to select what you think the most appropriate place for depositing my earthly remains." He and Julia would eventually be laid to rest in the grand monument in New York City now famously known as Grant's Tomb. As for funds resulting from the publication of his memoirs, he had already left instructions with Fred, his oldest child.

Most significantly, he told Julia, "Look after our dear children and direct them in the paths of rectitude." He would be terribly distressed, he said, if he thought that any one of the children would stray from the path of goodness, but he believed that they never had and never would.

And then, in a sentence that indicated his overriding love for Julia and his family he wrote, "With these few injunctions, and the knowledge I have of your love and affections, and of the dutiful affections of all our children, I bid you a final farewell until we meet in another, and I trust better, world."

He added a P.S. "This will be found in my coat after my demise."[11]

Grant completed his memoirs around July 20, 1885, and he died soon after on July 23, 1885. He died a painful death, but he did heroic work to complete his memoirs before he departed this earth. But how successful were Grant's memoirs? In early 1886, roughly six months after Grant's death,

Charles L. Webster wrote out a check to Julia Dent Grant to pay the first royalty to her from the publication of her husband's memoirs. It was the largest royalty check ever written up to that time—$250,000. And later Webster sent other payments which, together with the first royalty check, totaled nearly $450,000, or $11 million in modern money. As for the loan from Vanderbilt, it was never repaid. However, Grant insisted on providing Vanderbilt with collateral consisting of gifts he had received on his world tour. Vanderbilt eventually donated those gifts to the Smithsonian, never making any money on the transaction. Ulysses S. Grant left his wife more than enough money to survive, and his memoirs went on to become one of the most-praised books of nonfiction in American literature.[12]

AFTERWORD

ULYSSES S. GRANT, STEPHEN D. LEE, AND MISSISSIPPI STATE UNIVERSITY

Introductory Note

It is my great privilege as the nineteenth president of
Mississippi State University to share a personal reflection on
the unique relationship and enduring connection between
Ulysses S. Grant and Stephen D. Lee, who served from 1880
to 1899 as the first president of our 141-year-old institution.
—Mark E. Keenum

In the early twentieth century, two events—one held in
Vicksburg, Mississippi, and one in Galena, Illinois—illus-
trated a fascinating connection between Mississippi State
University and Ulysses S. Grant. These events both foreshadowed the relationship that would eventually become a reality
in the twenty-first century, and they both revolved around a
figure who would prove pivotal in the relationship between
Mississippi State University and the Ulysses S. Grant Association: Stephen D. Lee. To understand that relationship, one
must begin with Lee's own story.

Stephen Dill Lee was no relation to Civil War General
Robert E. Lee, nor was he a native Mississippian. He was
born in Charleston, South Carolina, in 1833. Two years later
he suffered the loss of his mother. His father remarried,
but the elder Lee's poor health made the family's economic

situation modest at best. Education was beyond the family's means, so Stephen D. Lee looked to the United States Military Academy for a free education. He proved to be a successful student there, graduating in the first half of his 1854 class, seventeenth out of forty-six. Upon graduation he was assigned to the artillery branch, his commission signed by Mississippian and future Confederate president Jefferson Davis, then the secretary of war under President Franklin Pierce.[1]

Lee served in the US Army in Texas, in Florida, and on the frontier. He did well, but then storm clouds began to fill the nation's skies. On February 20, 1861, some two months before Fort Sumter, he resigned his US Army commission, and the South Carolina governor made him a captain in that state's artillery service. Quickly Lee found himself in the middle of an upcoming war. On April 11, 1861, Confederate General P. G. T. Beauregard put three men (Lee; Colonel James Chesnut, the husband of Mary Chesnut of *Diary from Dixie* fame; and Chesnut's aide de camp) on a boat to Fort Sumter with a message to Union commander Major Robert Anderson, demanding surrender. Anderson refused, and artillery shells began to rain down on the fort in the middle of the Charleston harbor—according to some sources, on Lee's and Chesnut's orders. Anderson soon had to surrender. The Civil War was on.[2]

From that point on, Lee was an important officer in the Confederate army. He led Confederate soldiers during a variety of battles in both the Eastern and the Western Theaters. He fought at Seven Pines, the Seven Days, Malvern Hill, Second Bull Run, and Antietam. (In the Battle of Malvern Hill, my direct ancestor—Sergeant Milligan Keenum of the Twenty-Sixth Alabama—fought, was wounded, and later died in a Richmond military hospital.)

Ulysses S. Grant and Stephen D. Lee encountered each other in combat for the first time at Vicksburg. Although he was an artillery officer, Lee led an infantry division against William T. Sherman, who, on Grant's orders, had launched an unsuccessful attack at Chickasaw Bayou on the flank of the Walnut Hills, where Vicksburg was located. Then from January to May 1863, Lee was a brigade commander in the Department of Mississippi and Eastern Louisiana.

Lee served as artillery commander for the Confederate general overseeing the defense of Vicksburg, John C. Pemberton. Grant won out in the long struggle, and on July 4 he forced Pemberton to surrender the city. Like the other Confederates who fought at Vicksburg, Lee received a parole from Grant and had to promise, as they all did, that they would not get back into the war unless exchanged by a Union prisoner of equal rank. Lee signed that promise but then learned from the Confederate secretary of war that he had already been formally exchanged. So he went back to the war, this time commanding Confederate cavalry.[3]

Grant and Sherman heard that Lee had returned to the fight, but they did not know that he had been properly exchanged. Sherman reacted with concern because of his respect for Lee's ability. He referred to Lee as "the most enterprising of all in their army." Grant stated, "I do not think General Lee would act in bad faith," but instructed Sherman to look into the matter of the parole. When they learned in September 1863 that Lee had indeed been properly exchanged, they considered the matter resolved.[4]

Lee then saw combat against Sherman in the Atlanta campaign, against George H. Thomas at Nashville, and against Sherman again in the Carolinas campaign. As part of Joseph E.

Johnston's army, he surrendered to Sherman at Bennett Place, North Carolina, in 1865.

Stephen D. Lee's postwar experiences centered on his work in Mississippi. Near the end of the war, on February 8, 1865, he had married Regina (Lilly) Harrison of Columbus and for the next thirteen years worked as a farmer on her family's Mississippi land.

On February 1, 1878, Lee was elected Mississippi state senator. On February 28, 1878, he participated in the establishment of the Agricultural and Mechanical College of Mississippi. Lee was very popular among the state's farmers: he knew progressive agriculture and passionately believed that "revitalization of the region lay in industrial education for southern youth." As a result he was named the new school's first president and organized Mississippi A&M on the model of the United States Military Academy at West Point.[5]

Later Lee was one of the three-member park commission appointed by President William McKinley to insure that the Vicksburg National Military Park be established properly. This park is a monument to all the soldiers, North and South, who fought there, but the fact that Lee realized that this was the site of Grant's greatest triumph and still was the leader in establishing it, is significant. In fact, Lee resigned his position as president of his beloved Mississippi A&M so that he could join the commission. His fellow commissioners elected him their chairman, the first former Confederate officer to hold such a position.[6] Lee died in 1908 immediately after giving a speech to Union veterans in Vicksburg, speaking to four of the regiments he had fought there forty-five years earlier.

The connection between Stephen D. Lee and Ulysses S. Grant to Vicksburg is undeniable. Both men memorialized the pivotal events at Vicksburg in their own work after the war, but it is fascinating that their families continued to feel that connection to Mississippi and to one another even after their deaths. One example of this connection occurred in 1909, when Vicksburg saw the unveiling of a statue in Lee's honor on that battlefield. It was a marvelous occasion, filled with crowds, speeches, and old veterans. For such a grand event, there had to be a special keynote speaker, and the choice further emphasized the connection between Grant, Lee, and the state of Mississippi. The speaker was Frederick Dent Grant, the oldest son of Ulysses S. Grant. The 1917 commemoration of Grant's birth in Galena, Illinois, proved to be another example of these ties. The keynote speaker at that event was Blewett Lee, the only child of Stephen D. Lee.[7]

These anecdotes illustrate the desire on the part of the former Civil War combatants and their families to bring the nation back together after the death and destruction of the war. In many ways that attempt at reconciliation continues, as our nation strives to fulfill its great promise for all, and Mississippi State University is playing an integral part.

These connections between the Grant and Lee families foreshadowed the future relationship between Mississippi State University and Ulysses S. Grant that came about in the twenty-first century. After the greatest division our nation has ever seen, Stephen D. Lee helped build a new educational institution that to this very day looks to the future, while respectfully seeking to comprehend the past through innovative scholarship and research. The establishment of the Ulysses S. Grant Presidential Library at Mississippi State, and the Frank and Virginia Williams Collection of Lincolniana, created a new opportunity for the study of the Civil War not from a Northern or Southern perspective but appropriately from an American perspective.

We have a past that continues to resonate on our campus—a campus like many in the Deep South that was led by a former Confederate officer after the Civil War. But now this very same campus is home to the Grant Presidential Library and the Williams Collection of Lincolniana. These landmark collections serve as a bridge—a bridge connecting our history with a better present and a brighter future. Today, and for generations to come, it is my hope that they also stand as powerful symbols of reconciliation, unity, and humanity's ongoing journey toward understanding.

NOTES

INTRODUCTION

1. Edwina S. Campbell, *Citizen of a Wider Commonwealth: Ulysses S. Grant's Postpresidential Diplomacy* (Carbondale: Southern Illinois University Press, 2016), 36.

ONE. BIOGRAPHICAL SKETCH OF ULYSSES S. GRANT

1. The number of biographies written about U. S. Grant is large. A listing of books and articles about him can be found on the website of the Ulysses S. Grant Presidential Library, www.usgrantlibrary.org. A printed source is Marie Kelsey, *Ulysses S. Grant: A Bibliography* (Santa Barbara, CA: Praeger, 2005). This chapter is based on the variety of books and articles in these two sources.

2. Ulysses S. Grant, *The Personal Memoirs of Ulysses S. Grant: The Complete Annotated Edition*, ed. John F. Marszalek, with David S. Nolen and Louie P. Gallo (Cambridge, MA: Belknap Press of Harvard University Press, 2017), 14.

3. Grant, *Personal Memoirs*, 16–21.

4. Grant, *Personal Memoirs*, 21–23.

5. Grant, *Personal Memoirs*, 25.

6. Grant, *Personal Memoirs*, 27–31.

7. The two most recent biographies of Grant are Ron Chernow, *Grant* (New York: Pengiun, 2017) and Ronald C. White, *American Ulysses: A Life of Ulysses S. Grant* (New York: Random House, 2016).

8. The most comprehensive study of Grant's two-term presidency is Charles W. Calhoun, *The Presidency of Ulysses S. Grant* (Lawrence: University Press of Kansas, 2017).

9. John Russell Young, *Around the World with General Grant* (New York: American News Company, 1879).

10. Charles Bracelen Flood, *Grant's Final Victory: Ulysses S. Grant's Heroic Last Year* (New York: DaCapo, 2011); Joan Waugh, *U. S. Grant: American Hero, American Myth* (Chapel Hill: University of North Carolina Press, 2009), 262.

TWO. COLLEGE LIFE

1. Ulysses S. Grant, *The Personal Memoirs of Ulysses S. Grant: The Complete Annotated Edition*, ed. John F. Marszalek, with David S. Nolen and Louie P. Gallo (Cambridge, MA: Belknap Press of Harvard University Press, 2017), 21.

2. Joan Waugh, *U. S. Grant: American Hero, American Myth* (Chapel Hill: University of North Carolina Press, 2009), 15.

3. Hamlin Garland, *Ulysses S. Grant: His Life and Character* (New York: Doubleday, 1898), 21.

4. Albert D. Richardson, *A Personal History of Ulysses S. Grant* (Hartford, CT: American Publishing Company, 1868), 73.

5. Garland, *Ulysses S. Grant*, 24; Grant, *Personal Memoirs*, 16, 19; Waugh, *U. S. Grant*, 19.

6. Garland, *Ulysses S. Grant*, 25; Richardson, *Personal History*, 74.

7. Grant, *Personal Memoirs*, 17; Waugh, *U. S. Grant*, 17.

8. Richardson, *Personal History*, 49–50, 75; Waugh, *U. S. Grant*, 19.

9. Grant, *Personal Memoirs*, 16.

10. Richardson, *Personal History*, 86; Waugh, *U. S. Grant*, 20–21.

11. Richardson, *Personal History*, 91.

12. Grant, *Personal Memoirs*, 16.

13. Grant, *Personal Memoirs*, 21.

14. Waugh, *U. S. Grant*, 22.

15. Grant, *Personal Memoirs*, 22.

16. *Official Register of the Officers and Cadets of the U.S. Military Academy, West Point, New York. June, 1840* (New York: USMA Printing Office, 1840), 16; *Official Register . . . June, 1841*, 13; *Official Register . . . June, 1842*, 9; *Official Register . . . June, 1843*, 7.

17. *Official Register . . . June, 1840*, 16, 23; *Official Register . . . June, 1841*, 13, 20; *Official Register . . . June, 1842*, 21; *Official Register . . . June, 1843*, 7, 19.

18. Garland, *Ulysses S. Grant*, 51.

19. *Official Register . . . June, 1840*, 16; Grant, *Personal Memoirs*, 31–32; Grant to Albert E. Church, 1843, *The Papers of Ulysses S. Grant*, ed. John Y. Simon (Carbondale, IL: Southern Illinois University Press, 1967), 1:365.

20. Grant, *Personal Memoirs*, 21–22.

21. Ronald C. White, *American Ulysses: A Life of Ulysses S. Grant* (New York: Random House, 2016), 34–35.

THREE. THE EVILS OF SLAVERY

1. Ulysses S. Grant to Mary Grant, March 21, 1858, *The Papers of Ulysses S. Grant,* ed. John Y. Simon (Carbondale: Southern Illinois University Press, 1967), 1:341; Manumission of Slave document, March 29, 1859, *Papers of Ulysses S. Grant*, 1:347, 347n, 348n.

2. Willie Lee Rose, ed., *A Documentary History of Slavery in North America* (Athens: University of Georgia Press, 1999), 15–17.

3. See Josiah Priest, *Slavery, as It Relates to the Negro, or African Race: Examined in the Light of Circumstances, History and the Holy Scriptures; With an Account of the Origin of the Black Man's Color, Causes of His State of Servitude and Traces of His Character as well in Ancient as in Modern Times with Strictures on Abolitionism* (Albany: C. Van Benthuysen and Co., 1845).

4. An Address Setting Forth the Declaration of the Immediate Causes Which Induce and Justify the Secession of Mississippi from the Federal Union and the Ordinance of Secession (Jackson: Mississippian Book and Job Printing Office, 1861), 3.

5. Manisha Sinha, *The Slave's Cause: A History of Abolition* (New Haven: Yale University Press, 2016), 105–12.

6. John E. Kleber, ed., *The Kentucky Encyclopedia* (Lexington: University of Kentucky Press, 1992), 489.

7. Ulysses S. Grant, *The Personal Memoirs of Ulysses S. Grant: The Complete Annotated Edition*, ed. John F. Marszalek, with David S. Nolen and Louie P. Gallo (Cambridge, MA: Belknap Press of Harvard University Press, 2017), 8.

8. William F. McFeely, *Grant* (New York: W. W. Norton & Co., 1981), 8.

9. Byron Williams, *History of Clermont and Brown Counties, Ohio: From the Earliest Historical Times Down to the Present*, (Milford: Hobart

Publishing Co., 1913), 1:362; Enlistment document, September 14, 1839, *Papers of Ulysses S. Grant*, 1:3, 3n.

10. Robert McCorkle Magill, *Magill Family Record* (Richmond: R. E. Magil, 1907), 126–27; *Papers of Ulysses S. Grant*, 1:xxxvii; Brooks D. Simpson, *Ulysses S. Grant: Triumph Over Adversity, 1822–1865* (Minneapolis: Houghton Mifflin, 2000), 9.

11. Simpson, *Ulysses S. Grant*, 9.

12. Grant to Elihu B. Washburne, August 30, 1863, *Papers of Ulysses S. Grant*, 9:218.

13. Grant, *Personal Memoirs*, 28.

14. Lawrence O. Christensen, William E. Foley, and Gary Kremer, eds., *Dictionary of Missouri Biography* (Columbia: University of Missouri Press, 1999), 346.

15. Katharine T. Corbett, *In Her Place: A Guide to St. Louis Women's History* (St. Louis: Missouri Historical Society Press, 1999), 74–75; Ronald C. White, *American Ulysses: A Life of Ulysses S. Grant* (New York: Random House, 2016), 49.

16. See Dan Herzog, *Happy Slaves: A Critique of Consent Theory* (Chicago: University of Chicago Press, 1989).

17. Julia Dent Grant, *The Personal Memoirs of Julia Dent Grant (Mrs. Ulysses S. Grant)*, ed. John Y. Simon (New York: G. P. Putnam's Sons, 1975), 34.

18. *Papers of Ulysses S. Grant*, 1:xxxviii.

19. Grant to Frederick Dent, April 19, 1861, *Papers of Ulysses S. Grant*, 2:3.

20. Grant to Frederick Dent, April 19, 1861, *Papers of Ulysses S. Grant*, 2:4.

21. Grant, *Personal Memoirs*, 294.

22. Grant to Mary Grant, August 19, 1862, *Papers of Ulysses S. Grant*, 5:311.

23. Grant, *Personal Memoirs*, 377.

24. Grant, *Personal Memoirs*, 756, 760–61.

25. Grant to Gerrit Smith, July 28, 1872, *Papers of Ulysses S. Grant*, 23:211.

FOUR. JUST A TASTE OF LIQUOR

1. John A. Rawlins to Ulysses S. Grant, November 17, 1863, *The Papers of Ulysses S. Grant*, ed. John Y. Simon (Carbondale: Southern Illinois University Press, 1982), 9:475n.

2. An informative book on alcoholism in nineteenth-century America is W. J. Rorabaugh, *The Alcoholic Republic: An American Tradition* (New York: Oxford University Press, 1979).

3. Rorabaugh, *Alcoholic Republic*, 237–39.

4. Rorabaugh, *Alcoholic Republic*, 181–222; Jack S. Blocker Jr., *American Temperance Movements: Cycles of Reform* (Boston: Twayne, 1989), 12, 14; Alexis McCrossen, "Sabbatarianism: The Intersection of Church and State in the Orchestration of Everyday Life in Nineteenth-Century America," in *Religious and Secular Reform in America: Ideas, Beliefs, and Social Change*, ed. David K. Adams and Cornelis A. van Minnen (Edinburgh: Mainstream, 1999), 133–40.

5. Blocker, *American Temperance Movements*, 11–21; Rorabaugh, *Alcoholic Republic*, 187–211; McCrossen, "Sabbatarianism," 133–40.

6. A recent biography of Ulysses S. Grant that presents a fresh evaluation of his drinking habits is Ron Chernow, *Grant* (New York: Penguin, 2017).

7. Chernow, *Grant*, 67.

8. Chernow, *Grant*, 83–87.

9. Chernow, *Grant*, 86–87.

10. John F. Marszalek, *Commander of All Lincoln's Armies: A Life of General Henry W. Halleck* (Cambridge, MA: Belknap Press of Harvard University Press, 2004), 116, 122.

11. Michael B. Ballard, *Grant at Vicksburg: The General and the Siege* (Carbondale: Southern Illinois University Press, 2013), 45.

12. Michael B. Ballard, *U. S. Grant: The Making of a General, 1861–1863* (Lanham, MD: Rowman and Littlefield, 2005), 143.

13. Chernow, *Grant*, xxiii.

14. Mary A. Livermore, *My Story of the War* (New York: DaCapo, 1995), 316.

15. John A. Rawlins, undated endorsement, *Papers of Ulysses S. Grant*, 9:476n.

FIVE. FIGHTING THE WAR

1. Ulysses S. Grant, *The Personal Memoirs of Ulysses S. Grant: The Complete Annotated Edition*, ed. John F. Marszalek, with David S. Nolen

and Louie P. Gallo (Cambridge, MA: Belknap Press of Harvard University Press, 2017), 175.

2. Grant, *Personal Memoirs*, 179, 179n; Timothy B. Smith, *Shiloh: Conquer or Perish* (Lawrence: University Press of Kansas, 2014), 246.

3. Michael B. Ballard, *Vicksburg: The Campaign That Opened the Mississippi* (Chapel Hill: University of North Carolina Press, 2014), 24–25.

4. An informative study of the Vicksburg campaign, on which this chapter is based, unless otherwise indicated, is Ballard, *Vicksburg: The Campaign*.

5. Richard L. Kiper, *Major General John Alexander McClernand: Politician in Uniform* (Kent, Ohio: Kent State University Press, 1991).

6. Chester Hearn, *David D. Porter: The Civil War Years* (Annapolis, MD: Naval Institute Press, 1996).

7. Grant, *Personal Memoirs*, 30–31.

8. Timothy B. Smith, *The Real Horse Soldiers: Benjamin Grierson's Epic 1863 Civil War Raid through Mississippi* (Eldorado Hills, CA: Savas Beatie, 2018); Michael B. Ballard, *Pemberton: The General Who Lost Vicksburg* (Jackson: University Press of Mississippi, 1999); Craig L. Symonds, *Joseph E. Johnston: A Civil War Biography* (New York: Norton, 1993); William J. Cooper Jr., *Jefferson Davis, American* (New York: Knopf, 2010).

9. Peter Cozzens, *The Shipwreck of Their Hopes: The Battles of Chattanooga* (Champaign: University of Illinois Press, 1996).

10. Ronald C. White, *American Ulysses: A Life of Ulysses S. Grant* (New York: Random House, 2016), 328.

11. The best studies of the Virginia campaign between Grant and Robert E. Lee are the books in the multivolume series written by Gordon C. Rhea. His most recent volume is *On to Richmond: Grant and Lee*, June 4–15, 1864 (Baton Rouge: Louisiana State University Press, 2017).

12. Ulysses S. Grant to Robert E. Lee, April 19, 1865, *The Papers of Ulysses S. Grant*, ed. John Y. Simon (Carbondale: Southern Illinois University Press, 1985), 14:373–74.

13. Grant, *Personal Memoirs*, 175.

SIX. GRANT AND LINCOLN

1. Edward H. Bonekemper, *A Victor, Not a Butcher: Ulysses S. Grant's Overlooked Military Genius* (Washington, DC: Regnery, 2004), 80;

Elizabeth Keckley, *Behind the Scenes, Or, Thirty Years a Slave and Four Years in the White House* (New York: Penguin, 2005), 133–34.

2. David Work, *Lincoln's Political Generals* (Urbana and Chicago: University of Illinois Press, 2009), 1–5.

3. Ron Chernow, *Grant* (New York: Penguin Press, 2017), 211.

4. Chernow, Grant, 336–37.

5. Douglas R. Egerton, *Thunder at the Gates: The Black Civil War Regiments That Redeemed America* (New York: Basic Books, 2016), 253.

6. T. Harry Williams, *Lincoln and His Generals* (New York: Vintage Press, 2011), 301.

7. Ulysses S. Grant, *The Personal Memoirs of Ulysses S. Grant: The Complete Annotated Edition*, ed. John F. Marszalek, with David S. Nolen and Louie P. Gallo (Cambridge, MA: Belknap Press of Harvard University Press, 2017), 473.

8. Grant, *Personal Memoirs*, 752–53.

9. Ulysses S. Grant to Edwin M. Stanton, May 11, 1864, *The Papers of Ulysses S. Grant*, ed. John Y. Simon (Carbondale: Southern Illinois University Press, 1982), 10:422; Robert C. Plumb, *Your Brother in Arms: A Union Soldier's Odyssey* (Columbia and London: University of Missouri Press, 2011), 207.

10. Edwin M. Stanton to Ulysses S. Grant, March 3, 1865, *Papers of Ulysses S. Grant*, 14:91n; Ulysses S. Grant to Robert E. Lee, March 4, 1865, *Papers of Ulysses S. Grant*, 14:98.

11. Christian G. Samito, *Lincoln and the Thirteenth Amendment* (Carbondale: Southern Illinois University Press, 2015), 90–93; Grant, *Personal Memoirs*, 679–81.

12. Carl Sandburg, *Abraham Lincoln: The Prairie Years and the War Years* (San Diego: Harcourt, 2002), 373–74.

SEVEN. LET US HAVE PEACE

1. Roger A. Fischer, "A Pioneer Protest: The New Orleans Street-Car Controversy of 1867," *Journal of Negro History* 53, no. 3 (1968): 228–29.

2. Hans L. Trefouse, "The Acquittal of Andrew Johnson and the Decline of the Radicals," *Civil War History* 14 (June 1968): 153, 158–59; Eric Foner and Livia Mahoney, *America's Reconstruction: People and Politics after the Civil War* (Baton Rouge: Louisiana State University Press, 1999),

82–86; Joan Waugh, *U. S. Grant: American Hero, American Myth* (Chapel Hill: University of North Carolina Press, 2009), 112–22.

3. Foner and Mahoney, *America's Reconstruction*, 112.

4. John Erwin Hollitz, *Thinking about the Past: A Critical Thinking Approach to U.S. History* (New York: Cengage Learning, 2015), 330; Foner and Mahoney, *America's Reconstruction*, 112–19.

5. Jon Meacham, *The Soul of America: The Battle for Our Better Angels* (New York: Random House, 2018), 65; John Russell Young, *Around the World with General Grant* (New York: American News Company, 1879), 2: 360.

6. Frank J. Scaturro, *The Supreme Court's Retreat from Reconstruction: A Distortion of Constitutional Jurisprudence* (Westport, CT: Greenwood Press, 2000), 7–11.

7. Ulysses S. Grant to Congress, March 30, 1870, *The Papers of Ulysses S. Grant*, ed. John Y. Simon (Carbondale: Southern Illinois University Press, 1995), 20:130–31.

8. Waugh, *U. S. Grant*, 139; George C. Rable, *But There Was No Peace: The Role of Violence in the Politics of Reconstruction* (Athens: University of Georgia Press, 2007), 107; Hollitz, *Thinking about the Past*, 330.

9. Foner and Mahoney, *America's Reconstruction*, 124–25; Meacham, *Soul of America*, 66–67.

10. Foner and Mahoney, *America's Reconstruction*, 125, 128.

11. Foner and Mahoney, *America's Reconstruction*, 128.

12. Foner and Mahoney, *America's Reconstruction*, 128; Waugh, *U. S. Grant*, 120, 147–51.

13. Fischer, "A Pioneer Protest," 233.

EIGHT. GILDED AGE CORRUPTION

1. "St. Louis. Babcock's Arrival," *Chicago Daily Tribune*, Feb. 6, 1876.

2. Charles W. Calhoun, *The Presidency of Ulysses S. Grant* (Lawrence: University Press of Kansas, 2017), 9–10, 45.

3. Calhoun, *Presidency*, 43.

4. Jean Edward Smith, *Grant* (New York: Simon & Schuster, 2001), 461.

5. Calhoun, *Presidency*, 315–22.

6. Vincent P. De Santis, *The Shaping of Modern America: 1877–1920*, 3rd ed. (Wheeling, IL: Harlan Davidson, 1989), 80–82; Judy Hilkey, *Character*

Is Capital: Success Manuals and Manhood in Gilded Age America (Chapel Hill: University of North Carolina Press, 1997), 2–3, 10–11.

7. Calhoun, *Presidency*, 12.

8. Calhoun, *Presidency*, 12.

9. De Santis, *Shaping*, 43–44.

10. Calhoun, *Presidency*, 12.

11. Calhoun, *Presidency*, 83–84, 305, 321.

12. Ron Chernow, *Grant* (New York: Penguin, 2017), 672–79.

13. Calhoun, *Presidency*, 367–70.

14. Chernow, *Grant*, 819–20; Smith, *Grant*, 554, 586–87.

15. Mark Wahlgren Summers, *The Era of Good Stealings* (New York: Oxford University Press, 1998), 269.

16. Smith, *Grant*, 593–96.

17. Smith, *Grant*, 583–84.

18. Smith, *Grant*, 584.

19. Chernow, *Grant*, 803–4.

20. Calhoun, *Presidency*, 498–99, 524–25; Smith, *Grant*, 590–91.

21. Allan Nevins, *Hamilton Fish: The Inner History of the Grant Administration* (New York: Ungar, 1957), 798.

22. Calhoun, *Presidency*, 518–19, 522–23.

23. "The Trial of Gen. Babcock," *New York Times*, Feb. 13, 1876.

24. Smith, *Grant*, 590, 592.

25. Chernow, *Grant*, 807.

NINE. TOURING THE WORLD

1. Edwina S. Campbell, *Citizen of a Wider Commonwealth: Ulysses S. Grant's Postpresidential Diplomacy* (Carbondale: Southern Illinois University Press, 2016), 34–35.

2. Ulysses S. Grant to John F. Long, January 28, 1877, *The Papers of Ulysses S. Grant*, ed. John Y. Simon (Carbondale: Southern Illinois University Press, 2005), 28:142.

3. *Papers of Ulysses S. Grant*, xxiv; Rutherford B. Hayes to Ulysses S. Grant, December 25, 1876, *Papers of Ulysses S. Grant*, 28:106n; Grant to Rutherford B. Hayes, February 20, 1877, *Papers of Ulysses S. Grant*, 28:160; Campbell, *Citizen of a Wider Commonwealth*, 11–13.

4. *Papers of Ulysses S. Grant*, xxix–xxv.

5. Grant to Jesse Root Grant, Jr., *Papers of Ulysses S. Grant*, 28:199.

6. Julia D. Grant, *The Personal Memoirs of Julia Dent Grant (Mrs. Ulysses S. Grant)*, ed. John Y. Simon (New York: G. P. Putnam's Sons, 1975), 203.

7. Ron Chernow, *Grant* (New York: Penguin Press, 2017), 867; Julia Grant, *Memoirs*, 208–9; William S. McFeely, *Grant* (New York: W. W. Norton and Company, 1981), 458–59.

8. Ulysses S. Grant to Edward F. Beale, November 4, 1877, *Papers of Ulysses S. Grant*, 28:xxvi, 299.

9. *Papers of Ulysses S. Grant*, 28:xxvii.

10. Grant's Conversation with Otto von Bismarck, June 30, 1878, *Papers of Ulysses S. Grant*, 28:409.

11. *Papers of Ulysses S. Grant*, 28:xxvii–xxviii.

12. Grant's Travel Diary, January 23–July 26, 1879, *Papers of Ulysses S. Grant*, 29:86.

13. Grant to Prince Kung and Iwakura Tomomi, August 13, 1879, *Papers of Ulysses S. Grant*, 29:213–15.

14. Ronald C. White, *American Ulysses: A Life of Ulysses S. Grant* (New York: Random House, 2016), 609.

15. Campbell, *Citizen of a Wider Commonwealth*, 36.

TEN. A FINAL FAREWELL

1. The Battles and Leaders of the Civil War Series appeared in *Century Magazine*, November 1884 to November 1887. Later it was published in four volumes as Robert U. Johnson and Clarence Clough Buell, eds. *Battles and Leaders of the Civil War* (New York: Century Company, 1887–88).

2. Adam Badeau, *Military History of Ulysses S. Grant*, 3 vols. (New York: Appleton, 1885).

3. Ron Chernow, *Grant* (New York: Penguin, 2017), 915–27.

4. Robert U. Johnson, *Remembered Yesterdays* (Boston: Little Brown, 1923), 209–23.

5. Chernow, *Grant*, 930–37.

6. Chernow, *Grant*, 934–36.

7. Ulysses S. Grant, *The Personal Memoirs of Ulysses S. Grant: The Complete Annotated Edition*, ed. John F. Marszalek, with David S. Nolen

and Louie P. Gallo (Cambridge, MA: Belknap Press of Harvard University Press, 2017), xx–xxi.

8. A sketch of Harrison Terrell may be found in "Negro with a History," *Indianapolis Journal*, May 3, 1903; See also index to *The Papers of Ulysses S. Grant*, ed. John Y. Simon (Carbondale: Southern Illinois University Press, 2009), 31:485.

9. Grant, *Personal Memoirs*, xx–xxi.

10. Grant, *Personal Memoirs*, xxii.

11. Ulysses S. Grant to Julia Dent Grant, June 29, 1885, *Papers of Ulysses S. Grant*, 31:387–88.

12. Grant, *Personal Memoirs*, xxiv.

AFTERWORD. ULYSSES S. GRANT, STEPHEN D. LEE, AND MISSISSIPPI STATE UNIVERSITY

1. The modern biography of Stephen D. Lee is Herman Hattaway, *General Stephen D. Lee* (Jackson: University Press of Mississippi, 1976). An early short biography is Dabney Lipscomb, *General Stephen D. Lee: His Life, Character, and Services* (University, Mississippi: n.p. 1909). A brief overview is Albert Castel, "Stephen Dill Lee," in John A. Garraty and Mark C. Carnes, eds., *American National Biography* (New York: Oxford University Press, 1999), 13:403–4.

2. Hattaway, *General Stephen D. Lee*, 20–23.

3. Hattaway, *General Stephen D. Lee*, 98–100; G.O. No. 1, August 18, 1863, *War of the Rebellion, A Compilation of the Official Records of the Union and Confederate Armies*, 127 volumes (Washington DC: Government Printing Office, 1880–1901), volume 30, part 4, page 504.

4. William T. Sherman to Ulysses S. Grant, August 28, 1863; Grant to William T. Sherman, August 28, 1863; William T. Sherman to John A. Rawlins, September 17, 1863, *The Papers of Ulysses S. Grant*, ed. John Y. Simon (Carbondale, IL: Southern Illinois University Press, 1967), 9:205–6, 206n, 207n.

5. Hattaway, *General Stephen D. Lee*, 168–69, 178–92; John K. Bettersworth, *People's College: A History of Mississippi State* (University, AL: University of Alabama Press, 1953), 47–175; Michael B. Ballard, *Maroon and White, Mississippi State University, 1878–2003* (Jackson: University Press of Mississippi, 2008), 9–40.

6. Hattaway, *General Stephen D. Lee*, 224–33.

7. "Monument to Gen. Stephen D. Lee [June 11, 1909]" *Confederate Veteran* 17 (July 1909): 308–9; "Birthday of General U. S. Grant" *Journal of the Illinois State Historical Society* 19 (April 1917), 161–62.

FURTHER READING

ULYSSES S. GRANT

Ballard, Michael B. *Grant at Vicksburg: The General and the Siege.* Carbondale: Southern Illinois University Press, 2013.

Calhoun, Charles W. *The Presidency of Ulysses S. Grant.* Lawrence: University Press of Kansas, 2017.

Chernow, Ron. *Grant.* New York: Penguin, 2017.

Marszalek, John F., with David S. Nolen and Louie P. Gallo, eds. *The Personal Memoirs of Ulysses S. Grant. The Complete Annotated Edition.* Cambridge: Belknap Press of Harvard University Press, 2017.

Simon, John Y., and John F. Marszalek, eds. *The Papers of Ulysses S. Grant.* Carbondale: Southern Illinois University Press, 1967–2012. 32 volumes.

Smith, Jean Edward. *Grant.* New York: Simon and Schuster, 2001.

Waugh, Joan. *U. S. Grant: American Hero, American Myth.* Chapel Hill: University of North Carolina Press, 2009.

White, Ronald C. *American Ulysses: A Life of Ulysses S. Grant.* New York: Random House, 2016.

STEPHEN D. LEE

Hattaway, Herman. *General Stephen D. Lee.* Jackson: University Press of Mississippi, 1975.

Lipscomb, Dabney. *General Stephen D. Lee: His Life, Character, and Service.* N.p. 1909.

Thompson, John David. "Stephen D. Lee: P.A.C.S." MA thesis, University of Texas, 1950.

[Lee, Stephen D.] no title, collected in 1896, by "The Library," a book of newspaper clippings, presently located in Special Collections, Mitchell Memorial Library, Mississippi State University.

ABRAHAM LINCOLN

Basler, Roy P., ed. *The Collected Works of Abraham Lincoln.* 8 vols. New Brunswick, NJ: Rutgers University Press, 1953–1955.

Donald, David Herbert. *Lincoln.* New York: Simon and Schuster, 1995.

Fehrenbacher, Don E., ed. *Abraham Lincoln: Speeches and Writing. 1832–1865.* 2 vols. New York: Library of America, 1989.

Goodwin, Doris Kearns. *Team of Rivals: The Political Genius of Abraham Lincoln.* New York: Simon and Schuster, 2006.

Holzer, Harold. *Lincoln and the Power of the Press: The War for Public Opinion.* New York: Simon and Schuster, 2014.

Kerner, Fred, ed. *A Treasury of Lincoln Quotations.* New York: Doubleday, 1965.

Williams, Frank J. *Judging Lincoln.* Carbondale: Southern Illinois University Press, 2007.

Williams, Frank J. *Lincoln As Hero.* Carbondale: Southern Illinois University Press, 2012.

INDEX

ABOUT THE AUTHORS

John F. Marszalek, Giles Distinguished Professor Emeritus of History, Executive Director, Ulysses S. Grant Association and Ulysses S. Grant Presidential Library

David S. Nolen, Associate Professor, Mitchell Memorial Library and Associate Editor, Ulysses S. Grant Association and Ulysses S. Grant Presidential Library

Louie P. Gallo, Assistant Editor, Ulysses S. Grant Association and Ulysses S. Grant Presidential Library

Frank J. Williams, Chief Justice (Ret.) Rhode Island Supreme Court, President of the Ulysses S. Grant Association and donor of Frank J. and Virginia Williams Collection of Lincolniana, Mississippi State University

Mark E. Keenum, President, Mississippi State University